# The Quotable Traveler

# The Quotable Traveler

EDITED BY
DEBORAH McHugh

THE LYONS PRESS
Guilford, Connecticut
An imprint of The Globe Pequot Press

The Lyons Press is an imprint of The Globe Pequot Press.

Printed in the United States of America

10 9 8 7 6 5 4 3 2 1

Library of Congress Cataloging-in-Publication Data

The quotable traveler / edited by Deborah McHugh.
    p. cm.
Includes bibliographical references and index.
ISBN 1-58574-405-0
1. Travel—Quotations, maxims, etc.  I.  McHugh, Deborah.

IN6084.T7Q67 2001
910—dc21

2001050270

*To*
*my husband, James McHugh,*
*my father, Bernard Purcell,*
*my mother, Mary Trafton,*
*and my sister, Lisa Purcell,*
*with special mention to Rainy Swamp*

# Contents

# Introduction

Spread before me on my desk are the *New York Times* Travel section, opened to an article about Morocco; a map of Majorca alongside a guidebook to Madagascar; and next to them, a glossy four-color brochure of Monaco. As I push them all aside, postponing the tricky task of choosing my next destination, I wonder just what makes me want to travel. From that first time my mother packed my brother, my sister, and me into the car and headed to the Poconos to the last time my husband and I touched down in Prague, my urge to travel has never dimmed. The lure of visiting distant lands has held me fast—just as it holds so many others. Indeed, travel and tourism has become one of the world's largest industries. Every year, hundreds of millions of travelers pack their bags, lock up their homes, and set off for somewhere else. Just what is it that makes us all want to roam?

Of course, humans have always been nomads. Prehistoric hunters traveled because game didn't readily come to them—they had to pursue it. They traveled to survive. Ancient farmers migrated to other fields once they'd depleted the nutrients in the soil. They too traveled to survive. You might call these first travelers business travelers of a sort. They traveled not for pleasure or sightseeing, but out of necessity. Food, shelter, and climate were not so much chosen as discovered.

And even after populations began to settle in towns, some people still felt the need to wander. Traders set off, first on local and regional, then intercontinental and, finally, global trips, in the pursuit of exotic wares, great wealth, new territory, and personal glory. Medieval pilgrims waved farewell to home and family to spend months—even years—on the road, seeking salvation (and maybe a few religious relics to bring home as souvenirs). Later, wealthy young gentlemen would regularly spend months and years abroad on Grand Tours—ostensibly educative journeys, although they certainly proved enjoyable adventures as well.

Undoubtedly people traveled solely for the love of traveling before Englishman Thomas Cook's time, but it was in the 1840s that he realized travel could be packaged as a venture of holiday pleasure for the masses. Cook is credited with arranging the first trip for a group of people who didn't necessarily know each other. He more or less invented "tourism" as we know it: travel to numerous destinations during one trip for the sake of sightseeing.

As greater numbers of travelers set out to greater numbers of destinations, the complaint that nowhere in the world had been left untouched by tourism became common. And with the advent of air travel, the idea that the journey to a place is as much a part of the travel experience as the arrival (as put forth by so many early travel writers) lost much of its relevance. Even on a clear day, there is little below a person can recognize from 33,000 feet in the air; above the clouds, it's just one long monotonous, if panoramic, view. Air travel certainly has brought far away lands closer in time, but getting there has become tedious at best, and at its worst, robs the traveler of a sense of distance, a sense of the world's immensity.

Travel by sea retains some of that sense of journeying great distances, but many people now consider life aboard a modern cruise ship *the* vacation itself, with ports of call incidental. Luxurious trains, reminiscent of the glory days of the 1920s and 1930s, are making comebacks but, just as with cruise ships, it is not *where* you go so much as *how* you go. Well-appointed accommodations, abundant menus, and an array of activities are the essentials; pretty scenery is an added bonus.

The dilemma of choosing between going in style and just going still confronts many of us. Purists may feel that unless you pack light, throw away the itinerary, and just stick your thumb out on the road, you are missing the "authentic" travel experience. Tourists may prefer to pack heavy, grab the guidebooks, and head for the all-inclusive resort—a vacation is all they need. Yet the differing opinions on what constitutes a "real" travel experience simply highlights the very personal and idiosyncratic nature of travel. There are so many places to see and so many ways of getting there, that travel offers rewards to anyone who wants to leave home (and even those who want to remain in their armchairs).

So, off we go to the ends of the Earth—from the North Pole to the South Pole and all around the Equator—with quotations from some of the world's most articulate wanderers and writers. From the time of Homer down to the present, those who have journeyed both near and far left behind evocative, fascinating, and often funny observations of the trials and triumphs of travel.

Join Mark Twain, Jack Kerouac, Paul Theroux, Michael Palin, Graham Greene, Bill Bryson, and a host of others as they share their insights and inspired recollections of their travels around the globe.

# 1

# Wanderlust

Content to stay home, some people never travel. Others rarely travel very far; they are satisfied to visit the same seashore cottage or mountain cabin every year, relieved just to be away from the routine of regular life for a little while. But there are some of us who must move, who must travel, who are born with an insatiable desire to see new places, new people, and have new (sometimes dangerous) experiences.

These days, however, new experiences are only new to us as individuals—it has become nearly impossible to "go where no man has gone before." There are few—if any—places left on this planet where someone, sometime, has not ventured ahead of us. One California man's search to find a novel destination has even taken him *off* this planet, making him the first person to ever take a "space station vacation" (with a remarkably reasonable $20,000,000 tour package supplied by the Russians).

Yet even if you are a first-time visitor to the overdeveloped, overcrowded resorts of the Caribbean or a seasoned traveler sampling the accommodations of the remote Beijing to Moscow Trans-Asian Railway or an intrepid pioneer setting off to tour outer space, when you get that urge to take off, if you don't experience a rush of excitement when you pick up and go—you're *not* traveling, you're just moving around.

Travel spoils you for regular life.

> BILL BARICH
> *TRAVELING LIGHT* (1984)

If life is a journey, then the best journeys should be like life, and life goes up and down.

> TED SIMON
> *RIDING HIGH* (1984)

There is a third dimension to traveling, the longing for what is beyond.

> JAN MYRDAL
> *THE SILK ROAD* (1980)

In every poet's life there comes a time when he tears himself away from his mother and starts running.

> MILAN KUNDERA
> *LIFE IS ELSEWHERE* (1973)

Comes over one an absolute necessity to move. And what is more, to move in some particular direction. A double necessity then: to get on the move, and to know whither.

D. H. LAWRENCE (1885–1930)

For my part, I travel not to go anywhere, but to go. I travel for travel's sake. The great affair is to move.

ROBERT LOUIS STEVENSON
*TRAVELS WITH A DONKEY IN THE CÉVENNES* (1879)

Traveling is one way of lengthening life, at least in appearance.

BENJAMIN FRANKLIN (1706–1790)

He said he wanted to slow life up and quite rightly felt that by traveling he would make time move with less rapidity.

GRAHAM GREENE
*TRAVELS WITH MY AUNT* (1969)

I check the time on my watch, and realize that at this point it could be whatever time I want it to be. Japanese time, Indian time, New York time or London time—they're all the same at the Pole.

MICHAEL PALIN
*POLE TO POLE* (1992)

Time travels in divers paces with divers person. I'll tell you who Time ambles withal, who Time trots withal, who Time gallops withal, and who he stands still withal.

WILLIAM SHAKESPEARE
*AS YOU LIKE IT* (c. 1599)

Travelling is like flirting with life. It's like saying, "I would stay and love you, but I have to go; this is my station."

LISA ST. AUBIN DE TERÁN (1953– )

The consolation of travel is the control it offers to cowards: you get up and leave; you abandon people; there are fresh winds and fresh places for faulty egos to dilate in; there is a sort of enjoyment to the fear.

JULIAN EVANS
*TRANSIT IN VENUS* (1992)

———————

The real meaning of travel, like that of a conversation by the fireside, is the discovery of oneself through contact with other people, and its condition is self-commitment in the dialogue.

PAUL TOURNIER
*THE MEANING OF PERSONS* (1957)

———————

Traveling is seeing; it is the implicit that we travel by.

CYNTHIA OZICK
"ENCHANTERS AT FIRST ENCOUNTER," *NEW YORK TIMES*
17 MARCH 1985

What makes people travel? At its most basic, the desire to get *to* somewhere or to escape *from* somewhere. There are those in pursuit and those in flight.

IAN LITTLEWOOD
*SULTRY CLIMATES* (2001)

Men run away to other countries because they are not good in their own, and run back to their own because they pass for nothing in the new places. For the most part light characters travel.

RALPH WALDO EMERSON (1803–1882)

No road offers more mystery than the first one you mount from the town you were born to, the first time you mount it of your own volition, on a trip funded by your own coffee tin of wrinkled dollars.

MARY KARR
*CHERRY* (2000)

Full of the energy and enthusiasm of youth, the prospects of so hazardous an undertaking had no terror for us, as we had been married but a few months, it appealed to us as a romantic wedding tour.

CATHERINE HAUN, ON SETTING OFF ACROSS THE PLAINS FROM IOWA TO CALIFORNIA, 1849, QUOTED IN *WESTERING WOMEN*

There's an old saying that goes something like, "when the going gets tough, the tough go on holiday."

SIMON MAYLE
*THE BURIAL BROTHERS* (1996)

From my tender youth I had a great desire to see forraine Countries, not to get libertie . . . but to enable my understanding, which I thought could not be done so well by contemplation as by experience; nor by the eare or any sence so well, as by the eies.

*AN ITINERARY WRITTEN BY FYNES MORYSON, GENT.* (1617)

An Englishman is never at home except when he is abroad.

JAMES A. MICHENER
*THE DRIFTERS* (1971)

I never aspired to being a great traveller. I was simply a young man, typical of my age; we travelled as a matter of course. I rejoice that I went when the going was good.

EVELYN WAUGH
*WHEN THE GOING WAS GOOD* (1934)

To enrich the mind with knowledge, to rectify the judge-
ment, to remove the prejudices of education, to compose
outward manner, and in a word to form the complete gentle-
man.

> THOMAS NUGENT, ON THE PURPOSE OF A PERIOD OF TRAVEL IN A
> YOUNG ARISTOCRAT'S LIFE
> *THE GRAND TOUR* (1749)

---

We took this trip round the world on bicycles because we are
more or less conceited, like to be talked about, and see our
names in the newspapers.

> JOHN FOSTER FRASER
> *ROUND THE WORLD ON A WHEEL* (1899)

---

It was in 1893 that, for the first time in my life, I found myself
in possession of five or six months which were not heavily
forestalled, and feeling like a boy with a new half-crown, I

lay about in my mind, as Mr. Bunyan would say, as to what to do with them. "Go and learn your tropics," said Science.

MARY KINGSLEY
*TRAVELS IN WEST AFRICA* (1897)

The moment of arrival in a new continent is momentous.

V. S. PRITCHETT
*AT HOME AND ABROAD* (1989)

For in simple truth we had drifted hither by accident, with no excuse of health, or business, or any serious object whatever; and had just taken refuge in Egypt as one might turn to the Burlington Arcade or the Passage des Panoramas—to get out of the rain.

AMELIA B. EDWARDS
*A THOUSAND MILES UP THE NILE* (1877)

WORLD CRUISE

ON A VOYAGE
OF 132 DAYS
129 WERE SUNNY

I have one remark more, before I leave this damp part of the world . . .

DANIEL DEFOE
*TOUR THRO' THE WHOLE OF GREAT BRITAIN* (1724–26)

I'm leaving because the weather is too good. I hate London when it's not raining.

GROUCHO MARX (1895–1977)

Everyone knows it rains in England.

SUSAN ALLEN TOTH
*ENGLAND FOR ALL SEASONS* (1997)

The great travelers . . . tend to be obsessed people; only obsession would get them across the distances they cross, or carry them through the hardships they face. . . . They seldom attain and could perhaps not really afford wisdom, since wisdom, in most cases, would have kept them from ever setting out.

LARRY MCMURTRY
*ROADS* (2000)

Perhaps it's in our blood, maybe it's just in our history, but surely it's in the American vein to head out for some other place when home becomes intolerable, or merely when the distant side of the beyond seems a lure we can't resist.

WILLIAM LEAST HEAT-MOON
*BLUE HIGHWAYS* (1982)

Americans have always been eager for travel, that being how they got to the New World in the first place.

OTTO FRIEDRICH
*TIME* 22 APRIL 1985

For it is only when a man goes out into the world with the thought that there are heroisms all round him, and with the desire all alive in his heart to follow any which may come within sight of him, that he breaks away as I did from the life he knows, and ventures forth into the wonderful mystic twilight land where lie the great adventures and the great rewards.

SIR ARTHUR CONAN DOYLE
*THE LOST WORLD* (1912)

My father now and then sending me small sums of money, I laid them out in learning navigation, and other parts of the mathematics, useful to those who intend to travel, as I always believed it would be, some time or other, my fortune to do.

JONATHAN SWIFT
*GULLIVER'S TRAVELS* (1726)

My getting to travel and see the world I pinned on restlessness and good fortune.

EDDY L. HARRIS
*MISSISSIPPI SOLO* (1988)

The old hunger for voyages fed at his heart. . . . To go alone . . . into strange cities; to meet strange people and to pass again before they could know him; to wander, like his own legend, across the earth—it seemed to him there could be no better thing than that.

THOMAS WOLFE
*LOOK HOMEWARD ANGEL* (1929)

One travels like a golf ball, hopping from green to green.

JOHN GUNTHER
*INSIDE AFRICA* (1953)

I have changed my habits with the hemispheres, but there is still some internal rhythm that comes alive in April.

TONY HORWITZ
*ONE FOR THE ROAD* (1987)

Then came spring, the great time for traveling, and everybody in the scattered gang was ready to take one trip or the other.

JACK KEROUAC
*ON THE ROAD* (1959)

When April with his sweet showers
has pierced March to the root . . .
then people long to go on pilgrimages,
and palmers long to seek strange shores

and far-off shrines known in various lands
and, especially, from the ends of every shire
in England they come to Canterbury,
to seek the holy blissful martyr
who helped them when they were sick.

GEOFFREY CHAUCER
THE GENERAL PROLOGUE, *THE CANTERBURY TALES* (c. 1386)

[I] set out across Europe like a tramp—or, as I characteristi-cally phrased it to myself, like a pilgrim or a palmer, an errant scholar, a broken knight or the hero of *The Cloister and the Hearth!*

PATRICK LEIGH FERMOR (1915– )

I have carried the soldier's musket, the traveler's stick, the pilgrim's staff.

CHATEAUBRIAND (1768–1848)

We see in these swift and skillful travelers a symbol of our life, which seeks to be a pilgrimage and a passage on this earth for the way of heaven.

POPE PAUL VI, BLESSING 20,000 CARS, BUSES, TRUCKS AND MOTOR
SCOOTERS ASSEMBLED IN ST. PETER'S SQUARE
*NEWSWEEK* 13 APRIL 1964

A motorcycle the size of "Betty" would have been beyond the dreams of the craziest pack leader at the Ace Café . . . in the monochrome days of Rockers, Nortons, and Marianne Faithfull, when good was middle class, bad was misunderstood and the motorcycle offered the stark truth to a generation of inarticulate searchers.

TOM CUNLIFFE
*GOOD VIBRATIONS* (2001)

From Whitman to Steinbeck to Kerouac, and beyond to the restless broods of the seventies, the American road has

represented choice, escape, opportunity, a way to somewhere else. However illusionary, the road was freedom, and
the freest way to ride the road was hitchhiking.

> TOM ROBBINS
> *EVEN COWGIRLS GET THE BLUES* (1976)

Hitchhiking, among other virtues, forces you to converse
with people you'd otherwise cross the street to avoid.

> TONY HORWITZ
> *ONE FOR THE ROAD* (1987)

When I finally escaped from prep school, with a highly con-
ditional diploma, I immediately headed west, emulating my
hero Kerouac by hitchhiking.

> ROB SCHULTHEIS
> *FOOL'S GOLD* (2000)

There's going to be a rucksack revolution.

> JACK KEROUAC
> *THE DHARMA BUMS* (1958)

From the contents of the knapsack it was evident that this man had been an artist and poet in search of effects.

> SIR ARTHUR CONAN DOYLE
> *THE LOST WORLD* (1912)

But people remain unconvinced that anything momentous is left to be discovered by traveling.

> EDWARD HOAGLAND
> *THE TUGMAN'S PASSAGE* (1982)

And make no mistake. Whatever they tell you, they are all looking for something.

ROBERT ALDEN RUBIN, ON HIKERS ALONG THE APPALACHIAN TRAIL
*ON THE BEATEN TRACK* (2000)

Adventure-travel is any activity used as a conduit to observe, share, enjoy, suffer, encounter, or experience that which is outside the boundaries of one's own day-to-day life.

RANDY WAYNE WHITE
*THE SHARKS OF LAKE NICARAGUA* (1999)

Though I can see now that my travels as much as the act of writing were ways of escape.

GRAHAM GREENE
*WAYS OF ESCAPE* (1980)

Travel was an antidote to an overdose of stability.

BILL BARICH
*TRAVELING LIGHT* (1984)

When one realizes that his life is worthless he either com-
mits suicide or travels.

EDWARD DAHLBERG (1900–1977)

Travel is one of the saddest pleasures in life.

MADAME DE STAËL (1766–1817)

True and sincere traveling is no pastime, but it is as serious as
the grave.

HENRY DAVID THOREAU (1817–1862)

Traveling makes men wiser, but less happy.

THOMAS JEFFERSON (1743–1826)

———◆•◆•◆———

At the back of the adventure lay a curiosity for things in general which I had even as a child, and a desire, justified by the unusually harassing surroundings of my youth, to escape into an emptier, less fretful life.

FREYA STARK
*THE COAST OF INCENSE* (1953)

———◆•◆•◆———

He was an idealistic hobo and said, That's all there is to it, that's what I like to do, I'd rather hop freights around the country and cook my food out of tin cans and wood fires, than be rich and have a home or work.

JACK KEROUAC
*THE DHARMA BUMS* (1958)

Rich and happy as I was after my third voyage, I could not make up my mind to stay at home altogether.

"THE SEVEN VOYAGES OF SINBAD THE SAILOR"
*THE ARABIAN NIGHTS* (c. 1000)

I stayed but two months with my wife and family, for my insatiable desire of seeing foreign countries, would suffer me to continue no longer.

JONATHAN SWIFT
*GULLIVER'S TRAVELS* (1726)

Traveling always entails infidelity. You do your best to mask the feeling of sly triumph that comes with turning your back on home and all it stands for.

JONATHAN RABAN
*PASSAGE TO JUNEAU* (1999)

I was drunk with travel, dizzy with the import of it all, and indifferent to thoughts of home and family.

CHARLES KURALT
*A LIFE ON THE ROAD* (1990)

I had once spread my wings, and now that I had returned to my nest again, I was dissatisfied.

RICHARD HALLIBURTON
*THE GLORIOUS ADVENTURE* (1927)

For the goodman is not at home, he is gone a long journey.

PROVERBS 7:19

When I was very young and the urge to be someplace was on me, I was assured by mature people that maturity would cure the itch. . . . Now that I am fifty-eight perhaps senility will do the job. Nothing has worked. In other words, I don't improve, in further words, once a bum always a bum.

JOHN STEINBECK (1902–1968)

I have travelled, in one way or another, all my life. I have loved every moment of it, and fully intend to go on until I drop.

JOHN JULIUS NORWICH
*A TASTE FOR TRAVEL* (1985)

# 2

# Departures and Destinations

SOUTHERN PACIFIC LINES

going away

Travelers have always been confronted with myriad choices of where to go and how to get there, and the travelers quoted in this collection represent the full range of these possibilities. Some chose to go in style as pampered passengers of the famed Orient Express or the *Queen Mary*, while other travelers left home to drift wherever mood and opportunity pushed them. A few brave souls looked upon travel as a way to escape ordinary existence while testing their mettle. Their destinations were at the farthest corners of the globe, where they explored strange and sometimes harsh terrain. And there were those travelers who set specific goals for themselves—to journey around the world in eighty days, to circle the Earth following the Equator, to trek from the North Pole to the South, or to navigate the entire length of the Mississippi. There are mundane motivations recalled here, too—more than one traveler reported that they simply left home in search of better weather.

These travelers have traversed arid deserts, penetrated dense jungles, and basked on sunny beaches. To arrive at these many destinations, they used every mode of transport available, boarding planes, trains, and ships; paddling canoes;

riding wagons; and mounting horses and camels. They have revved up their motorcycles, peddled their bicycles, hopped into cars, campers, and busses, or simply set off on foot. Grueling adversity challenged some of them, but most of them faced no severe hardships; they only dealt with the usual petty inconveniences and frustrations of life on the road. Fortunately, these travelers kept accounts of the adventures they experienced after they snapped their bags shut, locked their doors, and departed for destinations known and unknown.

A man should be ever booted to take his journey.

MICHEL DE MONTAIGNE (1533–1592)

A journey of a thousand miles must begin with a single step.

LAO-TZU (c. 570–490 B.C.)

It began with an advertisement in the Agony Column of *The Times*.

PETER FLEMING, ON HIS INSPIRATION TO SET OUT ON A SOUTH AMERICAN JOURNEY
*BRAZILIAN ADVENTURE* (1933)

We packed our bags and said our good-byes. And off we went.

MIKE TIDWELL
*AMAZON STRANGER* (1996)

It was a bright Sunday morning in early June, the right time to be leaving home.

LAURIE LEE
*AS I WALKED OUT ONE MIDSUMMER MORNING* (1969)

I always love to begin a journey on Sundays, because I shall have the prayers of the church to preserve all that travel by land, or by water.

JONATHAN SWIFT
*MY LADY'S LAMENTATION* (1728)

We have all seen miniature rainbows about a ship's prow, but the *Spray* sprung out a bow of her own that day, such as I have never seen before. Her good angel had embarked on the voyage; I so read in the sea.

CAPTAIN JOSHUA SLOCUM
*SAILING ALONE AROUND THE WORLD* (1900)

Before liftoff we watched a remarkable documentary . . . for people who'd never been on a plane before. It explained, in excruciating detail, how to get up, how to sit down, how to use a tray table, how to use a toilet, and not to be frightened when the screen drops down to show the movie.

CRAIG NELSON
*LET'S GET LOST* (1999)

Most international flights have a certain sense of high spirits about them somewhere along the way, but not this plane.

GEORGIE ANN GEYER, REFERRING TO A FLIGHT TO MOSCOW
*WAITING FOR WINTER TO END* (1994)

In those now far-off days the traveling rich could actually be seen traveling: on trains, transatlantic liners, even in aeroplanes—how they contrive to move about now is a mystery.

ERIC NEWBY
*DEPARTURES AND ARRIVALS* (1999)

Whenever people tell me how passionately they desire to Get Away From It All, I think I know what is in their mind's eye. They see themselves riding off into the sunset, or paddling a canoe down the silver wake of the moon, . . . they see themselves, in fact, in terms of the silent film.

PETER FLEMING
*ONE'S COMPANY* (1934)

Own only what you can carry with you; know language, know countries, know people. Let your memory be your travel bag.

ALEKSANDR SOLZHENITSYN (1918– )

You'll never meet a traveler who, after five trips, brags, "Every year I pack heavier."

RICK STEVES
*EUROPE THROUGH THE BACK DOOR* (1998)

I wanted to get me a full pack complete with everything necessary to sleep, shelter, eat, cook, in fact a regular kitchen and bedroom right on my back . . .

JACK KEROUAC
*THE DHARMA BUMS* (1958)

I cannot go so fast as I would, by reason of this Burden that is on my back.

JOHN BUNYAN
*THE PILGRIM'S PROGRESS* (1678)

The suitcase was big, and it was heavy.

SUSAN HERRMANN LOOMIS
*ON THE RUE TATIN* (2001)

Each gadget was light and marvelously well designed, but when I tossed them together into a nylon sack they assumed the weight and shape of a cannonball.

THURSTON CLARKE
*EQUATOR* (1988)

I stood alone in the gutter with my laden Triumph in the black and rainy night, fumbling with my parcels and wondering where to pack them.

TED SIMON
*JUPITER'S TRAVELS* (1979)

The ladies had some feeling for
these men of heavy packs.

ANN E. PORTER
"THE BANISHMENT OF PEDDLERS," *GODEY'S* 37, October 1848

And he said unto them, take nothing for your journey, neither stores, nor scrips, neither bread, neither money: neither have two coats apiece.

LUKE 9:3

He who would travel happily must travel light.

ANTOINE DE SAINT-EXUPÉRY (1900–1944)

I travel light; as light that is, as a man can travel who will still carry his body around because of its sentimental value.

CHRISTOPHER FRY
THE LADY'S NOT FOR BURNING (1948)

I travel a great deal but I never wander.

TOM ROBBINS
ANOTHER ROADSIDE ATTRACTION (1972)

Not all those who wander are lost.

J. R. R. TOLKIEN (1892–1973)

All of us wanderers are made like this.

HERMANN HESSE (1877–1962)

Even aimless journeys have a purpose I suppose.

TONY HORWITZ
*ONE FOR THE ROAD* (1987)

A good traveller does not much mind the uninteresting places.

FREYA STARK
*ALEXANDER'S PATH* (1958)

We travel, perhaps, with a secret and absurd hope of setting foot on the Hesperides, of running our little boat up a creek and landing in the Garden of Eden.

D. H. LAWRENCE (1885–1930)

I should be dumb not to have inquired the road I was to journey; and if dumb there would be an end to my calling.

JAMES FENIMORE COOPER
*THE LAST OF THE MOHICANS* (1826)

Writers and travelers are mesmerized alike by knowing of their destinations.

EUDORA WELTY
*ONE WRITER'S BEGINNINGS* (1984)

Selecting the shortest route to her destination, Nancy deftly shifted gears and was off.

CAROLYN KEENE
*THE SECRET OF THE OLD CLOCK* (1930)

———•••••———

A traveler who leaves the journey open to the road finds unforeseen things come to shape it.

WILLIAM LEAST HEAT-MOON
*BLUE HIGHWAYS* (1982)

———•••••———

It's the one thing you say about going to the end of the road: when you start making your way back to civilization, you don't need a rearview mirror, ain't nothing gaining on you.

TIM CAHILL
*ROAD FEVER* (1991)

After many adventures which I need not describe, and after traveling a distance which I will not mention, in a direction which I withhold, we came at last to a tract of country which has never been described, nor, indeed, visited save by my unfortunate predecessor.

SIR ARTHUR CONAN DOYLE
*THE LOST WORLD* (1912)

Seeing new places always brings up the possibility of other new places.

FRANCES MAYES
*UNDER THE TUSCAN SUN* (1997)

I wonder where we shall all be next year . . .

COLONEL FRED BURNBY
*A RIDE TO KHIVA* (1877)

Whenever I tell my family where I'm off to next, in fact, my mom always has one question: "Why on earth would you want to go there?"

CRAIG NELSON
*LET'S GET LOST* (1999)

———•••••———

Wheresoever you go, go with all your heart.

CONFUCIUS (c. 551–479 B.C.)

———•••••———

My favorite thing is to go where I have never gone.

DIANE ARBUS (1923–1971)

All that travel agents ever sought to put in a folder fumed in Scott-King's mind that drab morning. He had left his coin in the waters of Trevi; he had wedded the Adriatic; he was a Mediterranean man.

EVELYN WAUGH
"SCOTT-KING'S MODERN EUROPE" (1947)

'50th Anniversary'
Cruise de Luxe
TO THE **Mediterranean**

Does this boat go to Europe, France?

ANITA LOOS (1888–1981)

When does this place get to England?

BEATRICE LILLIE (1898–1989), ON BOARD THE *QUEEN MARY*

When the ship goes wop (with a wiggle in between)
And the steward falls in the soup tureen . . .
Why then you will know (if you haven't guessed)
You're "Fifty north and forty yet!"

RUDYARD KIPLING
*JUST-SO STORIES* (1902)

So the Venice-Simplon Orient Express will not, today, visit either Venice or Simplon.

MICHAEL PALIN
*AROUND THE WORLD IN EIGHTY DAYS* (1989)

If you are lucky enough to have lived in Paris as a young man, then wherever you go for the rest of your life it stays with you, for Paris is a moveable feast.

ERNEST HEMINGWAY
*A MOVEABLE FEAST* (1964)

Ay, now am I in Arden; the more fool I: when I was at home, I was in a better place: but travelers must be content.

WILLIAM SHAKESPEARE
*AS YOU LIKE IT* (c. 1599)

Africa is a cruel country; it takes your heart and grinds it into powdered stone—and no one minds.

ELSPETH HUXLEY
*THE FLAME TREES OF THIKA* (1959)

I chant it out loud—Africa; again—Africa. The sound resonates within, as if I am a bell being struck—a call to my soul to awaken.

SUSANA HERRERA
*MANGO ELEPHANTS IN THE SUN* (2000)

When you have made up your mind to go to west Africa the very best thing you can do is to get it unmade again and go to Scotland instead.

MARY KINGSLEY
*TRAVELS IN WEST AFRICA* (1897)

Scotland, thank God, is not for everyone.

ROBIN DOUGLAS-HOME
"SCOTLAND: THE DOUR AND THE BEAUTIFUL," *VOGUE*
15 APRIL 1964

There was a kind of wonder, indeed, that England should be as English as, for my entertainment, she took the trouble to be.

HENRY JAMES
*ENGLISH HOURS* (1888)

Mrs. Bullen would never have come to Jashimpur at all had it not been for the failure of a love affair.

GERALD HANLEY, EXPLAINING WHY A TRAVELER WENT TO INDIA AND STAYED 40 YEARS
*THE JOURNEY HOMEWARD* (1961)

With an uncertain spot on my lungs, and feeling hopeless and ill, I went to the South Seas to get well. I did.

HECTOR MACQUARRIE
*TAHITI DAYS* (1920)

To depart is often more satisfying than to arrive unless you are the first on the scene.

ERIC NEWBY
*DEPARTURES AND ARRIVALS* (1999)

At last he reached the summit, and a wide and novel prospect burst upon him with an effect almost like that of the Pacific upon Balboa's gaze.

THOMAS HARDY
*FAR FROM THE MADDING CROWD* (1874)

In the Romantic Age, when the rule of taste was as yet un-challenged, conscientious travellers went to immense pains to insure that the vista or monument to which they were making pilgrimage should burst upon their properly condi-tioned gaze at precisely the right angle, the correct light.

OSBERT LANCASTER
*CLASSICAL LANDSCAPE WITH FIGURES* (1947)

If you do not expect it, you will not find the unexpected.

HERACLITUS (C. 537–475 B.C.)

Few visitors to Disneyland expect their lives to be changed by what they find there, and at the end of the week, after they've been beguiled, they climb back in their cars and drive home.

ROBERT ALDEN RUBIN
ON THE BEATEN TRACK (2000)

And because Epcot attracts people who would otherwise water down the cultures in the actual countries, I suppose— and I never thought I'd hear myself say this—Disney is true eco-tourism.

DOUG LANSKY
UP THE AMAZON WITHOUT A PADDLE (1999)

Before us were travel trailers parked in straight rows, with their little canopied portals and flowerpots, bicycles and outdoor barbecues.

PETER JENKINS
*ALONG THE EDGE OF AMERICA* (1995)

To many people holidays are not voyages of discovery, but a ritual of reassurance.

PHILIP ANDREW ADAMS
*AUSTRALIAN AGE* 10 SEPTEMBER 1983

The Epanchin family had at last made up their minds to spend the summer abroad, all except the general, who could not waste time in "travelling for enjoyment," of course.

FYODOR DOSTOEVSKY
*THE IDIOT* (1868)

[Tourists are] a very gloomy-looking tribe. . . . I have seen much brighter faces at a funeral than at the Plaza of St. Mark's. One wonders why they come abroad.

ALDOUS HUXLEY
*ALONG THE ROAD* (1925)

Come my friends.
'Tis not too late to seek a newer world.

ALFRED, LORD TENNYSON
"ULYSSES" (1842)

"Everything will go well," replied Candide. "I've already noticed that the sea of the New World is better than our European seas: it's calmer, and the winds are steadier. I'm sure it's the New World that is the best of all possible worlds."

VOLTAIRE
*CANDIDE* (1759)

If this is the best of all possible worlds, then where are the others?

TRISTAN JONES
*ENCOUNTERS OF A WAYWARD SAILOR* (1991)

At sea there is always a catch somewhere, as Columbus bitterly remarked on sighting America.

PETER FLEMING
*ONE'S COMPANY* (1934)

The road to Hades is easy to travel.

BION (C. 1ST OR 2nd CENTURY B.C.)

Travel, travel—never so much of it . . .

EDWARD HOAGLAND
*THE TUGMAN'S PASSAGE* (1982)

The globe is growing smaller by the day, and those of us alive at this moment can go to places our great-grandparents only dreamed about, at a speed and in a comfort they could not have imagined.

PICO IYER
"FIRST PERSON MIDDLE EAST: THE WORRY ZONE"
CONDE NAST TRAVELER May 2001

Covering great distances by train and boat restored my sense of the earth's immensity.

TIZIANO TENZANI
A FORTUNE TELLER TOLD ME (1997)

The world has shrunk, and I was able, now, to go to its uttermost part.

SARA WHEELER
TERRA INCOGNITA (1996)

Regardless of the wonders of technology and communications, our world is the same size as it ever was, and somewhere on its surface colorful, fascinating and unpredictable things are happening, just as they always have.

TED SIMON
*JUPITER'S TRAVELS* (1979)

———

In a world rapidly becoming homogenized through the proliferation of luxury hotels, mass tourism, and satellite communications fewer and fewer unsimulated adventures remain.

ROBERT D. KAPLAN
*BALKAN GHOSTS* (1997)

———

Tourism, human circulation considered as consumption is fundamentally nothing more than the leisure of going to see what has become banal.

GUY DEBORD (1931– )

I have come to know a part of the world where peak experiences seem to be the rule, not the exception, and where, frankly, I feel most alive.

JOHN WALDEN
*JUNGLE TRAVEL AND SURVIVAL* (2001)

———

Perhaps it's my natural pessimism, but it seems that an awfully large part of travel these days is to see things while you still can.

BILL BRYSON
*IN A SUNBURNED COUNTRY* (2000)

———

The big blank spaces in the map are all being filled in, and there's no room for romance anywhere.

SIR ARTHUR CONAN DOYLE
*THE LOST WORLD* (1912)

I had been searching for somewhere to go, somewhere that was not already suburbanised and where there was still something left to see that had not already been seen and described by hundred or thousands of my kind before me.

GAVIN MAXWELL
*A REED SHAKEN BY THE WIND* (1957)

When we were fully off again, we began, in a perfect fever, to strain our eyes for Rome; and when, after another mile or two, The Eternal City appeared, at length, in the distance; it looked like—I am half afraid to write the word—like LONDON!!!

CHARLES DICKENS
*PICTURES FROM ITALY* (1846)

Traveling, you realize that differences are lost: each city takes to resembling all cities, places exchange their form, order, distances, a shapeless dust cloud invades the continents.

ITALO CALVINO (1923–1985)

Discount airfares, a car in every parking space and the interstate highway system have made every place accessible—
and every place alike.

RONALD STEEL
"LIFE IN THE LAST 50 YEARS," *ESQUIRE* JUNE 1983

———•••———

I pity the man who can travel from Dan to Beersheba and
cry, 'tis all barren!

LAURENCE STERNE
*A SENTIMENTAL JOURNEY THROUGH FRANCE AND ITALY* (1768)

———•••———

Travel in the East is the occupation of your whole time, not a
mere passage from one place of residence to another.

ELIOT WARBURTON
*THE CRESCENT AND THE CROSS* (1845)

In this disjointed, rootless age, I've got a place. I'm the richest man in the world, even if it's only fool's gold in the end.

ROB SCHULTHEIS
*FOOL'S GOLD* (2000)

---

You are coming to learn that destination achieved is seldom what it promised when you first set off.

KEATH FRASER
*BAD TRIPS* (1991)

---

Without the journey there can be no destination.

BRIAN THOMPSON
"DECCAN," *GREAT RAILWAY JOURNEYS OF THE WORLD* (1981)

---

There's an amazing release that comes when you drive coast to coast, when you plug one ocean into another in your mind.

MICHAEL PATERNITI
*DRIVING MR. ALBERT* (2000)

An involuntary return to the point of departure is without doubt, the most disturbing of all journeys.

IAIN SINCLAIR

I think wherever your journey takes you, there are new gods waiting there, with divine patience—and laughter.

SUSAN M. WATKINS

At the age of thirty-five one needs to go to the moon, or some such place, to recapture the excitement with which one first landed at Calais.

EVELYN WAUGH
WHEN THE GOING WAS GOOD (1934)

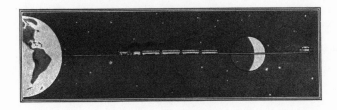

Why shouldn't someone take a trip to the moon someday?

JULES VERNE
*FROM THE EARTH TO THE MOON* (1865)

I didn't believe it was possible, but over the last few months, Space Adventures has made it a reality for me.

DENNIS TITO, ON SIGNING HIS CONTRACT TO FLY TO THE
INTERNATIONAL SPACE STATION

# 3

# On the Road

You may be the kind of traveler who leaves most of your belongings behind and with nothing more than a rucksack strapped to your back tramps solo around the world or you may be the kind who provides a vacation for nearly all your belongings—along with your whole family—by cramming them into an RV and hitting the highway. Yet however and with whomever you choose to travel, you share a common experience with many travelers. To walk, to jog, to hike, to drive, to sail, to fly—to be en route is the thing. The journey itself is as fulfilling as the ultimate arrival at your destination.

And once at your destination, there are still other journeys to make. When traveling in Arabia a camel may be your only transportation to an isolated desert oasis. Sailing down the Nile in a *felucca* is as natural as punting on the Thames. You can hot-air balloon over the Masai Mara plains of Kenya or dog sled along the frozen tundra of the Yukon. Yet, keep in mind, in India riding an elephant in a howdah may feel regal, but traveling down Main St. U.S.A. in one may get you a traffic ticket and a psychiatric consult. It's best to stick to the customs of the countries you visit.

To travel hopefully is a better thing than to arrive.

ROBERT LOUIS STEVENSON (1850–1894)

We travel in hope rather than certainty.

MICHAEL PALIN
*POLE TO POLE* (1992)

I am so anxious to get some place to stop and settle that my patience is not worth much.

LYDIA ALLEN RUDD, WRITING IN HER DIARY WHILE ON THE
OVERLAND TRAIL TO OREGON, 1852

Whither those roads led him he knew not. Either way there seemed to lie a great world full of chance and peril.

O. HENRY
"ROADS OF DESTINY" (1909)

Some parts of the world you make a conscious effort to visit and others have to wait until fate delivers you there.

TONY HAWKS
*ROUND IRELAND WITH A FRIDGE* (1998)

We've learned not to hesitate to take the unpaved roads if the route looks appealing.

FRANCES MAYES
*UNDER THE TUSCAN SUN* (1997)

The best paths usually lead to the most remote places.

SUSAN ALLEN TOTH
*MY LOVE AFFAIR WITH ENGLAND* (1992)

Traveler, there is no path; paths are made by walking.

ANTONIO MACHADO (1875–1939)

The swiftest traveler is he that goes afoot.

HENRY DAVID THOREAU (1817–1862)

It is no trick to go around the world these days . . . but to know it you have to crawl, to smell it and feel it between your toes. There is no other way. Not flying, not floating. You have to stay on the ground and swallow the bugs as you go. Then the world is immense.

TED SIMON
*JUPITER'S TRAVELS* (1979)

One day it occurred to me that it had been many years since the world had been afforded the spectacle of a man adventuresome enough to undertake a journey through Europe on foot. After much thought, I decided that I was the person fitted to furnish mankind with this spectacle.

MARK TWAIN
*A TRAMP ABROAD* (1880)

Distance changes utterly when you take the world on foot.

BILL BRYSON
*A WALK IN THE WOODS* (1998)

All told, the distance was about fifteen hundred miles. Could I walk it all? Why not? I thought.

TED SIMON
*THE GYPSY IN ME* (1997)

The first thing that struck me about walking across France was how easy it was.

MILES MORLAND
*WALKING ACROSS FRANCE* (1992)

I would travel on foot, sleep in hayricks in summer, shelter in barns when it was raining or snowing and only consort with peasants and tramps.

PATRICK LEIGH FERMOR
*A TIME OF GIFTS* (1977)

[The traveler's] sores shall gradually deepen themselves that they may heal inwardly, while he gives no rest to the sole of his foot, and at night weariness must be his pillow, that so he may acquire experience against his rainy days.

HENRY DAVID THOREAU (1817–1862)

I simply cannot understand the passion that some people have for making themselves thoroughly uncomfortable and then boasting about it afterwards.

PATRICIA MOYES (1923– )

There is a special ambivalence to journeys in which one's own discomfort seems mitigated by the awareness of the much greater misery of the people around one—though that mitigation adds another dimension of discomfort, the mental spasm of guilt.

GEORGE WOODCOCK
"MY WORST JOURNEY," *BAD TRIPS* (1991)

Ideally, traveling shouldn't involve guilt.

SUSAN ALLEN TOTH
*ENGLAND FOR ALL SEASONS* (1997)

It seems like an odd way to end a long walk, but getting a lift back is one of the treks of the trade, and I hike it like that.

DOUG LANSKY
*UP THE AMAZON WITHOUT A PADDLE* (1999)

Never again I vowed, would I try to hike the Appalachian Trail by car.

BILL BRYSON
*A WALK IN THE WOODS* (1998)

Everything in life is somewhere else, and you can get there in a car.

E. B. WHITE
*ONE MAN'S MEAT* (1943)

No longer the blasé driver of yesterday. You are the companion of a new kind of car—answering the call of the open country—yielding to the whims of the moment—a royal vagabond travelling the road to everywhere.

*JORDAN AUTOMOBILE COMPANY ADVERTISEMENT* (1920)

The interstate highway system is a wonderful thing. It makes it possible to go from coast to coast without seeing anything or meeting anybody.

CHARLES KURALT
*A LIFE ON THE ROAD* (1990)

There were days when I'd find myself hurtling down freeways toward receding destinations of evaporating worth, suspended between the fantastic and the mundane, between acclaim and abject defeat. Somehow, I'd missed the turnoff.

TONY COHAN
*ON MEXICAN TIME* (2000)

O public road, I say back I am not afraid to leave you, yet I love you, you express me better than I can express myself.

WALT WHITMAN (1819–1892)

We are always driving with our secrets in the trunk, amazed by the cows and rainbows and palm trees.

MICHAEL PATERNITI
*DRIVING MR. ALBERT* (2000)

For everyone coming to France directly from America, the first and most nerve-wracking shock to the system is traffic shock . . . menaced on all sides by small cars driven, it seemed, by bank robbers making a getaway.

PETER MAYLE
*ENCORE PROVENCE* (1999)

She liked to drive, and even liked being driven, but anything over seventy miles an hour made her feel hollow inside.

DOROTHY L. SAYERS
*BUSMAN'S HONEYMOON* (1937)

He had extracted himself from the Cambridge one-way system by the usual method, which involved going round and round it faster and faster until he achieved a sort of escape velocity and flew off at a tangent in a random direction.

DOUGLAS ADAMS
*DIRK GENTLY'S HOLISTIC DETECTIVE AGENCY* (1987)

The poetry of motion! The *real* way to travel! The *only* way to travel! Here today—in the next week tomorrow! Villages skipped, towns and cities jumped—always somebody else's horizons! O bliss! O poop-poop! O my! O my!

KENNETH GRAHAME
*THE WIND IN THE WILLOWS* (1908)

But when she looked down the highway there was not a single car in sight, the highway was hot and empty, which was awfully discouraging.

LARRY MCMURTRY
*THE DESERT ROSE* (1983)

I got to thinking Do I have to break down and buy me a bus ticket . . . ?

KEN KESEY, WITH KEN BABBS
*LAST GO ROUND* (1994)

"We could go home by bus," said Mama with a sigh.

GEORGES SIMENON
*THE WHITE HORSE INN* (1938)

I'd rather go by bus.

CHARLES, PRINCE OF WALES (1948– ), HIS ANSWER WHEN ASKED, AT
AGE SIX, IF HE WAS EXCITED ABOUT SAILING ON THE ROYAL YACHT

I wish that those Scenicruisers would be discontinued. . . .
Simply knowing that they are hurtling somewhere on this
dark night makes me most apprehensive.

JOHN KENNEDY TOOLE
*A CONFEDERACY OF DUNCES* (1980)

I had sneaked into San Francisco ... coming 3000 miles ... in a pleasant roomette on the California Zephyr train watching America roll by outside my private picture window ... all so easy and dreamlike compared to my old harsh hitch hiking before I made enough money to take transcontinental trains.

JACK KEROUAC
*BIG SUR* (1962)

You wake up in the morning your watch says it is eight o'clock; but you are travelling east, and you know that it is really nine, though you might be hard put to explain why this is so.

PETER FLEMING
*ONE'S COMPANY* (1934)

I always seem to have chosen the most eccentric and decrepit ways of getting to places.

MICHAEL WOOD
"ZAMBEZI EXPRESS," *GREAT RAILWAY JOURNEYS OF THE WORLD* (1981)

A private railroad car is not an acquired taste. One takes to it immediately.

ELEANOR R. BELMONT
*THE FABRIC OF MEMORY* (1957)

I'm rather disappointed at the lack of princesses, murderers and deposed heads of Europe.

MICHAEL PALIN, ABOUT HIS FELLOW TRAVELERS ON THE
ORIENT EXPRESS
*AROUND THE WORLD IN EIGHTY DAYS* (1989)

For three days these people, these strangers to one another, are brought together. They sleep and eat under one roof, they cannot get away from each other. At the end of their days they part; they go their separate ways, never perhaps to see each other again.

AGATHA CHRISTIE
*MURDER ON THE ORIENT EXPRESS* (1933)

Not all the early delights of train travel have gone, it seems. Here you can still nibble at the pleasures which were once the prerogative of the rich and famous.

ERIC ROBSON
"CHANGING TRAINS," *GREAT RAILWAY JOURNEYS OF THE WORLD*
(1981)

The Simplon-Orient. . . . finally ceased to run in May 1977, by which time it was infested with *malviventi* who drugged and robbed the passengers and subjected them to even worse indignities, which was the end of it.

ERIC NEWBY
*DEPARTURES AND ARRIVALS* (1999)

In the train, however fast it traveled, the passengers were compulsorily at rest; useless between walls of glass to feel emotion, useless to try to follow any activity except of the mind; and that activity could be followed without fear of interruption.

GRAHAM GREENE
*THE STAMBOUL TRAIN* (1932)

---

Travel can be one of the most rewarding forms of introspection.

LAWRENCE DURRELL
*BITTER LEMONS* (1957)

---

It wasn't as if you were traveling at all.

THEODORE DREISER, ON RIDING ON AN ENGLISH TRAIN
*A TRAVELER AT FORTY* (1913)

When the whistle blew and the call stretched thin across the night, one had to believe that any journey could be sweet to the soul.

CHARLES TURNER
*THE CELEBRANT* (1982)

There's nothing so dark as a railroad track in the middle of the night.

JAMES M. CAIN
*DOUBLE INDEMNITY* (1936)

Only a masochist (or railway fan) would really prefer the belching smoke, flying black smuts and rattling ride of the old steam trains to the smooth swiftness of the electrics which almost unnoticably accelerate to 100 miles an hour before we've even passed Wembley Stadium.

MICHAEL PALIN
"CONFESSIONS OF A TRAIN SPOTTER," *GREAT RAILWAY JOURNEYS OF THE WORLD* (1981)

The great if obvious feature of a train, as compared to a hotel room, is that your view is constantly changing.

BILL BRYSON
*IN A SUNBURNED COUNTRY* (2000)

But the sweetest way to me is a ship's upon the sea . . .

RUDYARD KIPLING (1865–1936)

———•••••———

When one turns forty and faces one's first transatlantic voyage, it is a more portentous event than when it comes at twenty.

THEODORE DREISER
*A TRAVELER AT FORTY* (1913)

———•••••———

On such a voyage, with its eternal monotonies, people's intellects deteriorate; the owners of the intellects soon reach a point where they almost prefer childish things to things of maturer degree.

MARK TWAIN, ON WHY DUNKING FIRST-TIME CROSSERS OF THE
EQUATOR IS SO AMUSING TO SHIP PASSENGERS
*FOLLOWING THE EQUATOR* (1897)

The *Queen Elizabeth II* provides vast amounts of entertainment for an age that has forgotten how to amuse itself unaided.

HANS KONING
*INTERNATIONAL HERALD TRIBUNE* 15 NOVEMBER 1985

After nine days . . . I'd gotten used to the horizon, to the orderly rhythm of the ship, and all of a sudden the world came flooding back. I found myself looking at Nova Scotia and thinking about my mortgage.

SARAH BALLARD
*SPORTS ILLUSTRATED* 1 OCTOBER 1984

Life onboard the *Oceanien* was like some terrible bed-sitting-room marriage. Almost everything formed grounds for divorce . . . I was either in a stupor or furious.

HUGO WILLIAMS
"LA FOLIE ANGLAISE," *ALL THE TIME IN THE WORLD* (1966)

Oh! ye state-room sailors, who make so much ado about a fourteen-days' passage across the Atlantic; who so pathetically relate the privations and hardships of the sea, where, after a day of breakfasting, lunching, dining off five courses, chatting, playing whist, and drinking champagne-punch, it was your hard lot to be shut up in little cabinets of mahogany and maple, and sleep for ten hours, with nothing to disturb you but "those good-for-nothing tars, shouting and tramping overhead,"—what would ye say to our six months out of sight of land?

HERMAN MELVILLE
TYPEE (1846)

I had taken a third-class or deck-passage, whereby the evils of the journey were exacerbated.

SIR RICHARD BURTON
PERSONAL NARRATIVE OF A PILGRIMAGE TO AL-MADINAH AND
MECCAH (1855–6)

## *A Night Afloat On A Wonder Boat!*
### To LOS ANGELES

I don't want to be like one of those old codgers one sees on the Cunard traveling first-class and complaining of the caviar.

GRAHAM GREENE
*TRAVELS WITH MY AUNT* (1969)

---

I shall never forget the one-fourth serious and three-fourths comical astonishment, with which, on the morning of the

third of January eighteen-hundred-and-forty-two, I opened
the door of, and put my head into, a "state-room" on board
the Britannia steam-packet . . .

CHARLES DICKENS, ON THE SHOCK HE RECEIVED WHEN HE SAW HOW
TINY ROOMS WERE ABOARD SHIP
*AMERICAN NOTES* (1842)

Of all the sorry places on earth one might have elected to be
caught in that February forenoon, it seemed to me that mine
was easily the most wretched. To recline at full length in a
wicker chair three miles off the coast of Borneo, shielded
from the tropical sun by a snowy ship's awning and caressed
by the vagrant airs of the west monsoon, and, in between
cooling draughts of lime squash tempered with a little gin, to
contemplate the plight of my friends in New York was as
painful an experience as any I have ever endured.

S. J. PERELMAN
*THE SWISS FAMILY PERELMAN* (1950)

The ocean was always an adventure in the unexpected.

JAMAKE HIGHWATER
*JOURNEY TO THE SKY* (1978)

---

Half the passengers, expiring from the indescribable agony which the rolling of the ship inflicts on the nerves and humors of the body, shaken in different directions, were so weakened that they lacked even the strength to become alarmed at their danger. The other half were shrieking and praying.

VOLTAIRE, DESCRIBING A VOYAGE TO LISBON.
*CANDIDE* (1759)

---

The prospect of getting to shore seemed vague.

HECTOR MACQUARRIE
*TAHITI DAYS* (1920)

---

I love to sail forbidden seas and land on barbarous coasts.

HERMAN MELVILLE (1819–1891)

Gray-eyed Athena sent them a favorable breeze, fresh wet wind, singing over the wine-dark sea.

HOMER (C. 700 B.C.)

—•••—

I wanted to sail beyond the sunset. I wanted to follow Ulysses' example and fill life once more to overflowing.

RICHARD HALLIBURTON
*THE GLORIOUS ADVENTURE* (1927)

—•••—

Evidence that the equator is a natural feature is so convincing that some people are fooled into "seeing" it.

THURSTON CLARKE
*EQUATOR* (1988)

—•••—

An elderly lady and her son, recreation-seekers from Massachusetts, had wandered westward, further and further from home, always intending to take the return track, but always concluding to go still further . . . Then they could go around the world, or go back the way they had come; the distance and the accommodations and outlay of time would be just the same, whichever of the two routes they might elect to take.

MARK TWAIN
*FOLLOWING THE EQUATOR* (1897)

I've gone as far as I can go, which was precisely my goal: to travel as close as possible to the exact other side of the planet from the place I call home.

MIKE TIDWELL
*IN THE MOUNTAINS OF HEAVEN* (2000)

This, he realized, was about as close to home as he was likely to get. Which meant that he was about as far from home as he could possibly be.

DOUGLAS ADAMS
*MOSTLY HARMLESS* (1992)

A "Bummel". . . I should describe as a journey, long or short, without an end; the only thing regulating it being the necessity of getting back within a given time to the point from which one started.

> JEROME K. JEROME
> *THREE MEN ON A BUMMEL* (1900)

Different forms of transport—ships, coaches, trains, planes—have long been favourite sites for pornography.

> IAN LITTLEWOOD
> *SULTRY CLIMATES* (2001)

Four hoarse blasts of a ship's whistle still raise the hair on my neck and set my feet to tapping.

> JOHN STEINBECK
> *TRAVELS WITH CHARLEY* (1962)

I love rivers.

ERIC NEWBY
*SLOWLY DOWN THE GANGES* (1966)

What would be waiting for me on the river? Kindness or evil? Beauty or savagery? Whatever, I don't want to miss a thing.

EDDY L. HARRIS
*MISSISSIPPI SOLO* (1988)

Without a doubt running the Amazon was the looniest thing I've ever done. I felt relieved when we finished and happy to get home afterwards.

JOE KANE
*RUNNING THE AMAZON* (1989)

He who rides the sea of the Nile must have sails woven of patience.

WILLIAM GOLDING
*AN EGYPTIAN JOURNAL* (1985)

The charm of these river voyages is their monotony.

V. S. PRITCHETT
*AT HOME AND ABROAD* (1989)

————•••••————

The sky is more impersonal than the sea.

TOM ROBBINS
*STILL LIFE WITH WOODPECKER* (1980)

————•••••————

In the air, you can eat, drink, sleep, talk on the phone, work on the computer, read books or magazines, have sex in the bathroom, and watch movies and TV. As far as I can see, it's just like being at home.

CRAIG NELSON
*LET'S GET LOST* (1999)

On a plane . . . you can pick up more and better people than on any other public conveyance since the stagecoach.

ANITA LOOS
*NEW YORK TIMES* 26 APRIL 1973

———•••••———

I must fly 100,000 miles a year, yet I have accumulated only about 212 air miles divided among twenty-three airlines.

BILL BRYSON
*I'M A STRANGER HERE MYSELF* (1999)

———•••••———

To say the plane was experiencing turbulence was like saying Michael Jordan can shoot an okay game of hoop.

MIKE TIDWELL
*IN THE MOUNTAINS OF HEAVEN* (2000)

No one seemed alarmed, so I practiced breathing evenly and holding up the airplane by the armrests.

FRANCES MAYES
*UNDER THE TUSCAN SUN* (1997)

Airline travel fractures my equanimity.

TIM CAHILL
*ROAD FEVER* (1991)

And then the idea of not flying for a whole year was as atrocious in itself.

TIZIANO TENZANI
*A FORTUNE TELLER TOLD ME* (1997)

Exit according to rule, first leg and then head. Remove high heels and synthetic stockings before evacuation: Open the door, take out the recovery line and throw it away.

RUMANIAN NATIONAL AIRLINES, EMERGENCY EVACUATION INSTRUCTIONS

A railroad station? That was sort of a primitive airport, only you didn't have to take a cab 20 miles out of town to reach it.

RUSSELL BAKER
*NEW YORK TIMES* 5 NOVEMBER 1986

If airport traffic continues to snarl, the only sure way to get there on Tuesday will be to leave on Monday.

DAVID PAULY
"AIRPORT '84: STALLED OUT," *NEWSWEEK* 30 JULY 1984

The sooner you are there, the sooner you will find out how long you will be delayed.

SHELLEY BERMAN (1926– )

The limitless jet-lag purgatory of Immigration and Baggage at Heathrow.

MONICA DICKENS
"A MODERN DICKENS WRITES ABOUT RETURNING TO THE LAND OF HER GREAT-GRANDFATHER," *CHRISTIAN SCIENCE MONITOR* 13 MARCH 1986

The Jet Age is crucifying the hobo because how can he hop a jet freight?

JACK KEROUAC
"THE VANISHING HOBO," *LONESOME TRAVELER* (1960)

When it comes to flying, I am a nervous passenger but a confident drinker and Valium-swallower.

MARTIN AMIS
"EMERGENCY LANDING," *SOHO SQUARE II* (1989)

The helicopter . . . approaches closer than any other [vehicle] to fulfillment of mankind's ancient dreams of the flying horse and the magic carpet.

IGOR SIKORSKY, ON THE 20TH ANNIVERSARY OF THE INITIAL FLIGHT OF HIS INVENTION
*NEW YORK TIMES* 13 SEPTEMBER 1959

It's wonderful to climb the liquid mountains of the sky. Behind me and before me is God and I have no fears.

HELEN KELLER (1880–1968), ON HER FLIGHT AROUND THE WORLD AT AGE 74

It was the most wonderful flight of my life. I reclined in the plane in a happy daze, occasionally glancing out the window just to remind myself of the distances we were traveling. No one had spit on my feet or vomited next to me. It was warm. The seats were soft.

STUART STEVENS
*NIGHT TRAIN TO TURKESTAN* (1988)

What we see and smell will probably make us sick.

MACKINLAY KANTOR
*THE CHILDREN SING* (1973)

———•◦•◦•———

Foreigners cannot enjoy our food, I suppose, any more than we can enjoy theirs.

MARK TWAIN
*A TRAMP ABROAD* (1880)

———•◦•◦•———

Our journeys have taught us the wisdom of the Esquimaux appetite, and there are few among us who do not relish a slice of raw blubber, or a chunk of frozen walrus beef.

ELISHA KENT KANE, M.D.
*ARCTIC EXPLORATIONS* (1853)

I was obligated to cultivate relations with the cuisine of the establishment.

HENRY JAMES
*A LITTLE TOWN IN FRANCE* (1884)

———

Eating in the Arab manner required to be learnt, and at the beginning I found it humiliatingly impossible.

GAVIN MAXWELL
*A REED SHAKEN BY THE WIND* (1957)

———

In foreign parts, so it is said, the pampered guts of Americans, then Scandinavians, are those most easily undone by local germs, due to the fanatical hygiene in our countries.

PETER MATTHIESSEN
*AFRICAN SILENCES* (1991)

It was useless to worry about the diseases I might catch, but sometimes it was difficult not to feel squeamish about the food and water.

WILFRED THESINGER
*THE MARSH ARABS* (1964)

We eat everything we see on the street. . . . Every few days one of us is ill with the *turistas*.

TONY COHAN
*ON MEXICAN TIME* (2000)

When we recovered from our illness we investigated how the food was prepared.

JOHN FOSTER FRASER
*ROUND THE WORLD ON A WHEEL* (1899)

# Pre-arranged Comfort

## on your trip in Europe

Dinner it was true had been revolting . . .

MILES MORLAND
*A WALK ACROSS FRANCE* (1992)

———•+++•———

To the infected travelers, food that once seemed exotic becomes a foul depot of mired flies and suspicious meats. The
native language, which once resembled a warbling flute, becomes a deafening chorus of barking frogs.

RANDY WAYNE WHITE
*THE SHARKS OF LAKE NICARAGUA* (1999)

———•+++•———

The "Food Question" has been solved by a modified rejec-
tion of all advice.

ISABELLA BIRD
*UNBEATEN TRACKS IN JAPAN* (1880)

It was John Hemming, Director of the National Geographic Society, who advised me that a true explorer never turns down a meal. It may be the last he'll be offered for days.

MICHAEL PALIN
*AROUND THE WORLD IN EIGHTY DAYS* (1989)

Six waiters in turn asked what I would like to order. There was a sweetness to this, since everyone forgot out of politeness to show me the day's menu.

JULIAN EVANS
*TRANSIT IN VENUS* (1992)

Be a loner, travel, talk to waiters only, in fact, in Milan, Paris, just talk to waiters.

JACK KEROUAC
*BIG SUR* (1962)

Soviet restaurants exist for one purpose, and that is to keep the customer out, and if by any chance he or she should get in to make life so uncomfortable that they wish they hadn't.

MICHAEL PALIN
*POLE TO POLE* (1992)

---

There are no taverns, no alehouses, nor stews among them . . .

THOMAS MORE
"OF THE TRAVELLING OF THE UTOPIANS," *UTOPIA* (1516)

Some years ago, I stayed at a country-house hotel so welcoming and convivial that I forgot to pay my check before leaving.

LINDSAY HUNT
*FODOR'S EXPLORING IRELAND* (2001)

We tarried overnight at a summer hotel . . . the Grand Hôtel des Bains. The word Grand means nothing in this connection; it has no descriptive value. On the Continent, all hotels, inns, taverns, hash houses, and slop troughs employ it. It is tiresome. This one was a good-enough hotel, and comfortable, but there was nothing grand about it but the bill, and even that was not extravagant enough to make the title entirely justifiable.

MARK TWAIN
"LETTERS TO SATAN" (1923)

As a general rule, it is advisable to frequent none but the leading hotels in places off the beaten track of tourists, and to avoid being misled by the appellation of "Grand-Hotel," which is often applied to the most ordinary inns.

KARL BAEDECKER
SOUTHERN FRANCE: HANDBOOK FOR TRAVELLERS (1907)

The Ritz is not ritzy.

CHARLES RITZ

———•••———

The bedrooms are just large enough for a well-behaved dwarf and a greyhound on a diet.

JOHN RUSSELL, ON MODERN EUROPEAN HOTELS
*NEW YORK TIMES* 4 AUGUST 1977

———•••———

I've always thought a hotel ought to offer optional small animals. . . . I mean a cat to sleep on your bed at night, or a dog of some kind to act pleased when you come in. You ever notice how a hotel room feels so lifeless?

ANNE TYLER
*THE ACCIDENTAL TOURIST* (1985)

The great advantage of a hotel is that it is a refuge from home life.

GEORGE BERNARD SHAW (1856–1950)

———•••———

In the hotel there was staying also a Polish count (you must know that ALL travelling Poles are counts!).

FYODOR DOSTOEVSKY
*THE GAMBLER* (1867)

———•••———

I never like to travel with people. I'm very much an individualist, and I can only really see things when I'm by myself. I've always had this thought that, in order to really feel everything and not miss things, one had to be by oneself.

GEORGIE ANN GEYER
*WAITING FOR WINTER TO END* (1994)

The man who goes alone can start today; but he who travels with another must wait till that other is ready.

HENRY DAVID THOREAU (1817–1862)

———•◦•◦•———

But the travel is lonely from here on.

TONY HORWITZ
*ONE FOR THE ROAD* (1987)

———•◦•◦•———

Neither sleepy nor deaf men are fit to travel quite alone. It is remarkable how often the qualities of wakefulness and watchfulness stand every party in good stead.

SIR FRANCIS GALTON
*THE ART OF TRAVEL* (1867)

It was as a solitary traveler that I began to discover who I was
and what I stood for.

PAUL THEROUX
*FRESH AIR FIEND* (2000)

It was my first day alone on a journey I had contemplated for
so long, and I was feeling joyfully rewarded.

TED SIMON
*THE GYPSY IN ME* (1997)

The journey in itself had no terrors for her; and she began it
without either dreading its length or feeling its solitariness.

JANE AUSTEN
*NORTHANGER ABBEY* (1818)

There were moments traveling with Ann when I expended great energy contemplating exotic ways of doing away with her.

STUART STEVENS
*MALARIA DREAMS* (1989)

When we wanted to change our plans, we consulted only each other and our own whims.

SUSAN ALLEN TOTH
*MY LOVE AFFAIR WITH ENGLAND* (1992)

And whosoever shall compel thee to go a mile, go with him twain.

MATTHEW 8:41

Journeys, like artists, are born and not made. A thousand differing circumstances contribute to them, few of them willed or determined by the will—whatever we may think.

LAWRENCE DURRELL
BITTER LEMONS (1957)

———◦•••◦———

The traveller's ambition often exceeds his powers of endurance.

KARL BAEDECKER
SWITZERLAND: HANDBOOK FOR TRAVELLERS (1899)

———◦•••◦———

The trips convinced me that as long as the rewards of the world outstripped those of my imagination, I might as well keep traveling.

BILL BARICH
TRAVELING LIGHT (1984)

4

# Travel Advisory

"Don't drink the water!" is the best-known universal precaution and number one reason why so many Americans are afraid to leave the country. And if they still contemplate setting off on a journey, they will also be warned: "Beware pickpockets," "Watch your passport," "Beware the unsolicited helpful guide," "Stay within well-defined tourist areas," and "Don't feed the animals."

There has never been a shortage of advice for travelers. As well as firsthand guidance from returning adventurers, handbooks that point out potential perils and guidebooks that point out worthy sights have long been bookstore staples. You can know where to stay, what to eat, and what hazards might confront you before you ever reach your destination.

Yet, in spite of the myriad warnings and guidance available to travelers, there are always foolhardy ones. They gorge on foods they know will make them ill, they head to major sightseeing attractions during high season, or get angry when the locals don't speak English. When homesickness overtakes them, they blame it on their host country.

Wise travelers take advice, but also learn to make their own way in strange places. They sample local foods, they visit fresh sights, and they make new friends. They travel neither in fear nor in a fog—and return home with their own bits of advice to share.

Without fear, travel has no meaning.

KEATH FRASER
*BAD TRIPS* (1991)

———•·•·•———

My people have always been anxious about traveling. I think this dates back to the Babylonian Exile.

DAVID MAMET
"A FAMILY VACATION," *WRITING IN RESTAURANTS* (1986)

———•·•·•———

In Bokonon, it is written that "peculiar travel suggestions are dancing lessons from God."

TOM ROBBINS
*ANOTHER ROADSIDE ATTRACTION* (1972)

———•·•·•———

Don't drink the water.

ANONYMOUS

Always go to the bathroom when you have a chance.

GEORGE V (1865–1936)

———•••••———

The single most important conclusion after having spent three weeks traveling through Japan, as well as countless hours reading, studying, and analyzing this fascinating culture, is that you should always tighten the cap on your shampoo bottle before you put it in your suitcase.

DAVE BARRY
*DAVE BARRY DOES JAPAN* (1992)

———•••••———

Is forbidden to steal towels, please. If you are not person to do such is please not to read notice.

SIGN IN TOKYO HOTEL

A towel, it says, is about the most massively useful thing an interstellar hitchhiker can have.

DOUGLAS ADAMS
*THE HITCHHIKER'S GUIDE TO THE GALAXY* (1979)

The traveller is cautioned against sleeping in chalets, unless absolutely necessary.

KARL BAEDECKER
*SWITZERLAND: HANDBOOK FOR TRAVELLERS* (1899)

Recognize tourist traps.

RICK STEVES
*EUROPE THROUGH THE BACK DOOR* (1998)

After a lifetime of travel he settled here on the Costa del Sol and told us there were five rules for successful travel. Never eat in any restaurant named Mom's. Never play poker with

anyone named Doc. Get your laundry done at every opportunity. Never refuse sex. And order any dish containing wild
rice.

JAMES A. MICHENER
*THE DRIFTERS* (1971)

Don't Panic.

DOUGLAS ADAMS
*THE HITCHHIKER'S GUIDE TO THE GALAXY* (1979)

Remember that the attraction of traveling by camel should
be tempered by the reality of debilitating heat and the potential for injury; it makes this mode of transportation dicey
at best.

ROBERT YOUNG PELTON
*THE WORLD'S MOST DANGEROUS PLACES* (1997)

Thou art a swift dromedary traversing her ways.

JEREMIAH 2:23

*Eliminate Travel Worry*

A camel makes an elephant feel like a jet plane.

JACQUELINE KENNEDY (1929–1994)

———•◦•◦•———

One tries in vain to imagine a crime for which the *piene forte et dure* of sixteen hours on a camel-back would not be a full and sufficient expiation.

MRS. AMELIA B. EDWARDS
*A THOUSAND MILES UP THE NILE* (1877)

Envelope please. And the winner of the Worthless Mode of
Transportation Award goes to . . . the ostrich!

DOUG LANSKY
*UP THE AMAZON WITHOUT A PADDLE* (1999)

But the ride was a "fearful joy," *if* a joy at all.

ISABELLA BIRD
*THE GOLDEN CHERSONESE* (1883)

In bygone times travel in Europe was made hateful and hu-
miliating by the wanton difficulties, hindrances, annoyances,
and vexations put upon it by ignorant, stupid, and disoblig-
ing transportation officials, and one had to travel with a
courier or risk going mad.

MARK TWAIN
"LETTERS TO SATAN" (1923)

It would often seem as if the railway companies did everything in their power to prevent people from using their lines.

AUGUSTUS J. C. HARE
NORTH-EASTERN FRANCE (1890)

Scott-King was hungry, weary and dispirited for he was new
to the amenities of modern travel.

EVELYN WAUGH
"SCOTT-KING'S MODERN EUROPE" (1947)

As Mr. Baedecker requests all tourists to call his attention to
any error which they may find in his guide-books, I dropped
him a line to inform him that when he said the foot-journey
from Wäggis to the summit was only three hours and a quar-
ter, he had missed it by just about three days.

MARK TWAIN
A TRAMP ABROAD (1880)

Go, little book, God send thee good passage,
And specially let this be thy prayere
Unto them all that thee will read or hear,
Where thou art wrong, alter their help to call,
Thee to correct in any part or all.

> KARL BAEDECKER
> *EGYPT AND THE SÛDÂN: HANDBOOK FOR TRAVELLERS* (1914)

My travels through this land, traced on a map, would look like the doodling of a kid with a crayon in his paw; circle upon circle upon circle.

> DAVE CARTY
> *BORN AGAIN AT THE LAUNDROMAT* (1992)

The passengers were curious to examine the moon during their journey; to facilitate their scrutiny of the new world they decided to take Beer and Moedler's excellent map, the

*Mappa Selenographica,* printed in four sheets and rightly re-garded as a masterpiece of observation and patience.

JULES VERNE
*FROM THE EARTH TO THE MOON* (1865)

I had three maps, and after two of them brought me to the verge of a breakdown I gave up and looked out the window.

SARA WHEELER
*TRAVELS IN A THIN COUNTRY* (1999)

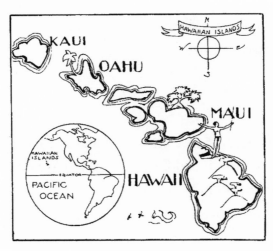

If you're lost, take out a map and look lost. You'll get help.

RICK STEVES
*EUROPE THROUGH THE BACK DOOR* (1998)

Unfortunately for us, we misread the map.

MICHAEL PATERNITI
*DRIVING MR. ALBERT* (2000)

Never go into the jungle without a compass.

MICHAEL CRICHTON
*TRAVELS* (1988)

She could teach him in earliest childhood no less than this, to find a home in his saddle, and to love old Homer, and all that old Homer sung.

A. W. KINGLAKE
*EOTHEN* (1844)

Homer would be my guide; the *Odyssey* my book.

RICHARD HALLIBURTON
*THE GLORIOUS ADVENTURE* (1927)

———•••••———

The *Guide* was something sacred and special.

DOUGLAS ADAMS
*MOSTLY HARMLESS* (1992)

———•••••———

A guide book is a queer thing.

MARK TWAIN
*A TRAMP ABROAD* (1880)

The traveler should never omit visiting any object of interest whenever it happens to be within his reach at the time, as he can never be certain what impediments may occur to prevent him from carrying his intentions into effect at a subsequent period.

MURRAY'S HANDBOOK FOR TRAVELLERS IN THE IONIAN ISLANDS, GREECE, TURKEY, ASIA MINOR AND CONSTANTINOPLE (1840)

You wouldn't have had time. You would always mean to go, but you never would go.

HENRY JAMES
THE AMERICAN (1877)

I am particular dating this letter, in hopes that every English traveller may avoid this place I write from.

CAPTAIN PHILIP THICKNESSE
A YEAR'S JOURNEY THROUGH FRANCE AND PART OF SPAIN (1777)

Even traveling despondently is better than arriving here.

DOUGLAS ADAMS
*MOSTLY HARMLESS* (1992)

———•••••———

It ought to be part of our patriotic feeling to endeavour to convey as agreeable an idea as possible of ourselves to those countries which we honour with our distinguished presence in our little trips.

MRS. C. E. HUMPHRIES
*MANNERS FOR WOMEN* (1897)

———•••••———

I sometimes wonder if two thirds of the globe is covered in red carpet.

CHARLES, PRINCE OF WALES (1948– )

They'll like you because you're a foreigner. They love foreigners; it's just strangers they hate.

JONATHAN RABAN
*OLD GLORY* (1981)

The attitude to foreigners is like the attitude to dogs: Dogs are neither human nor British, but so long as you keep them under control, give them their exercise, feed them, pat them, you will find their wild emotions are amusing, and their characters interesting.

V. S. PRITCHETT
*LONDON PERCEIVED* (1962)

An English tourist will always do well to remember that his approval or his custom is of no consequence whatever to an hotel-keeper in a quiet French town.

AUGUSTUS J. C. HARE
*NORTH-EASTERN FRANCE* (1890)

Foreign visitors are not encouraged.

MICHAEL PALIN
*POLE TO POLE* (1992)

———•·••·•———

Dress impressively like the French, speak with authority like the Germans, have blond hair like the Scandinavians and speak of no American presidents except Lincoln, Roosevelt and Kennedy.

SYLVAINE ROUY NEVES, ON HOW TO GAIN RESPECT WHILE TRAVELING IN EUROPE
*NEW YORK TIMES* 30 SEPTEMBER 1984

———•·••·•———

A few simple conjuring tricks, and a knowledge of how to show them off, are often of the highest use to travelers in winning the esteem and respect of their temporary hosts.

H. H. JOHNSTON
*HINTS ON OUTFITS* (1889)

Funny how tourism can get people to do things they would never do at home.

DOUG LANSKY
*UP THE AMAZON WITHOUT A PADDLE* (1999)

The *Turks* make great use of baths, we do not.

LORD BALTIMORE
*A TOUR TO THE EAST* (1767)

I was forced to affect peculiar local customs which embarrassed me terribly.

ALEXANDRA DAVID-NÉEL
*MY JOURNEY TO LLASA* (1927)

A frank, joking, but determined manner, joined with an air of showing more confidence in the good faith of the natives than you really feel, is the best.

SIR FRANCIS GALTON
*THE ART OF TRAVEL* (1867)

———•••••———

Give offence to no one, the prospective traveller is advised, for you will only get the worst of it.

LOUISE COLLIS
*MEMOIRS OF A MEDIEVAL WOMAN: THE LIFE AND TIMES OF MARGERY KEMPE* (1964)

———•••••———

It used to be said that the best way to ensure good health was to keep the pores of the skin open and the mouth shut!

*ASPINALL'S POCKET GUIDE TO THE WEST INDIES* (1907)

If the outlandish person come alone to strange nomad booths, let him approach boldly, and they will receive him.

CHARLES MONTAGU DOUGHTY
*TRAVELS IN ARABIA DESERTA* (1888)

I was well acquainted with the gag that if you looked like your passport picture, you needed a trip. I was unprepared for the preponderance of thuglike pictures which I found in the course of processing passports.

FRANCES G. KNIGHT, DIRECTOR, PASSPORT DIVISION,
U.S. STATE DEPARTMENT
*NEW YORK HERALD TRIBUNE* 21 FEBRUARY 1957

When you look like your passport photo, it's time to go home.

ERMA BOMBECK (1927–1996)

If you look like your passport picture, you're too ill to travel.

ANONYMOUS

Everything, it said, was against the travellers, every obstacle imposed alike by man and by nature.

JULES VERNE
*AROUND THE WORLD IN EIGHTY DAYS* (1873)

———•·•···•———

Travel is a bitter harassment, a purgatory of little exasperating annoyances, a ceaseless and pitiless punishment—I mean to an irascible man who had no business capacity and is confused by details.

MARK TWAIN
*A TRAMP ABROAD* (1880)

———•·•···•———

For a man on vacation, I had been unusually fretful.

MICHAEL CRICHTON
*TRAVELS* (1988)

Truthfully, I am "homesick" for a land that is not mine.

ALEXANDRA DAVID-NÉEL (1868–1969)

Homesickness is nothing. . . . Fifty percent of the people of the world are homesick all the time.

JOHN CHEEVER
"THE BELLA LINGUA" (1982)

And I dreamed of home long ago in New England, my little kitkats trying to go a thousand miles following me on the road across America, and my mother with a pack on her back, and my father running after the ephemeral uncatchable train . . .

JACK KEROUAC
THE DHARMA BUMS (1958)

If something terrible had happened to us on our trip I would of course be writing a different kind of article. But bad things can happen anywhere at any time.

PICO IYER
"FIRST PERSON MIDDLE EAST: THE WORRY ZONE,"
CONDE NAST TRAVELER MAY 2001

———◦•⊪•◦———

To put in mildly, I did not feel comfortable about the whole trip.

GEORGIE ANN GEYER
WAITING FOR WINTER TO END (1994)

It was surprisingly simple to leave—a departure rather than an escape.

JAMES HILTON, ON LEAVING SHANGRI-LA.
*LOST HORIZON* (1933)

The hallucinatory frenzy of departure has its result in a pitiable monotony. One changes his décor, not his existence.

JEAN PAUL ARON
*NEW YORK TIMES* 4 AUGUST 1986

I have just been all round the world and have formed a very poor opinion of it.

SIR THOMAS BEECHAM (1879–1961)

*Lucky!*

to go to Europe
in the fall

5

# Travelers, Tourists, and Wanderers

With so many millions of people setting off each year for other places, it is not surprising that there is a variety of traveler stereotypes. There are those who label themselves "real" travelers, priding themselves on being a hard, adaptable breed. They know the real pleasures and hardships of the journey, avoid the hackneyed tourist traps, and get to know the customs of the lands they visit. For them, travel is a metaphysical experience, not a mere diversion.

But then there are those others . . . the "tourists." "Real" travelers scoff at these amateurs. They wear big hats, big sunglasses, big shorts, big sneakers, and big tee shirts that advertise some other destination to which they've been. Their cameras clicking, their voices loud, they impose themselves on the landscape on bicycles, in cars, RVs, tour busses, and cruise ships. And they are as conspicuous in their bewilderment as they are in their dress. Poring over maps and guidebooks, they block parking lots, street corners, intersections, entryways, and cafeterias. They need to know what each moment of the trip will hold. They are as unlike as it is possible to be from that other group of travelers—those footloose wanderers who set off with neither itinerary nor agenda. Maybe these are the real travelers—the ones who go just for the sake of going.

There's no doubt about it: the easier it becomes to travel, the harder it is to be a traveller.

JOHN JULIUS NORWICH
*A TASTE FOR TRAVEL* (1985)

Travel is now impossible; tourism is all we have left.

PAUL FUSSELL (1924– )

"Tourists?" I was outraged. "You call me a *tourist*?"

KEN KESEY, WITH KEN BABBS
*LAST GO ROUND* (1994)

Travelers without some goal, some small quest, a bit of business to accomplish are tourists.

TIM CAHILL
*ROAD FEVER* (1991)

Like most people who don't own Bermuda shorts, I'm bored by ordinary travel.

> P. J. O'ROARKE
> *HOLIDAYS IN HELL* (1988)

The ideal traveler is a temperate man, with a sound constitution, a digestion like an ostrich, a good temper, and no race prejudices.

> WILLIAM HENRY CROSSE, M.D.
> *MEDICAL HINTS* (1906)

I believe I have a sunny disposition and am not naturally a grouch. It takes a lot of optimism, after all, to be a traveler.

> PAUL THEROUX
> *FRESH AIR FIEND* (2000)

The ability to see the bright side when times get rough may be an asset more valuable than physical conditioning.

JOHN WALDEN
*JUNGLE TRAVEL AND SURVIVAL* (2001)

That image came to me again and again, the image of an abandoned traveler—the worst fate for travelers is that they become lost and instead of revelling in oblivion, they fret and fall ill.

BRUCE CHATWIN AND PAUL THEROUX
*NOWHERE IS A PLACE* (1985)

I came to London. It had become the center of my world and I had worked hard to come to it. And I was lost.

V. S. NAIPAUL
*AN AREA OF DARKNESS* (1964)

If any man was to go among them that had some extraordinary talent, or that by much travelling had observed the customs of many nations (which made us to be so well received), he would receive a hearty welcome, for they are very desirous to know the state of the whole world.

THOMAS MORE
"OF THE TRAVELLING OF THE UTOPIANS," *UTOPIA* (1516)

Anyone who has traveled a little knows that the warmest reception an American will receive will come in Havana or Hanoi or among our ostensible enemies in Libya or Iran, where people are more than able to distinguish between foreign governments they distrust and foreign individuals they only want to befriend.

PICO IYER
"FIRST PERSON MIDDLE EAST: THE WORRY ZONE,"
*CONDE NAST TRAVELER* MAY 2001

He who is only a traveler learns things at second-hand and by the halves, and is poor authority.

HENRY DAVID THOREAU (1817–1862)

The perfect traveler does not know his destination.

LAO-TZU (c. 570–490 B.C.)

The flâneur—that aimless stroller who loses himself in the crowd, who has no destination and goes wherever caprice or curiosity directs his steps.

EDMUND WHITE
THE FLÂNEUR (2001)

That's why tourists come here, to see what nowhere looks like. And if you want to see nowhere, you have to start somewhere.

MICHAEL FRAYN
"THE LONG STRAIGHT," GREAT RAILWAY JOURNEYS OF THE WORLD (1981)

That word, "American," is usually spoken by outsiders with strange anticipation, as if, at any moment, they expect me to do something unusual or entertaining.

RANDY WAYNE WHITE
*THE SHARKS OF LAKE NICARAGUA* (1999)

Every Englishman abroad, until it is proved to the contrary, likes to consider himself a traveller and not a tourist.

EVELYN WAUGH
*WHEN THE GOING WAS GOOD* (1934)

A speck in the broad tracts of Asia remained still impressed with the mark of patent portmanteaus and the heels of London boots.

A. W. KINGLAKE
*EOTHEN* (1844)

Most Orientals regard the European traveller as a Croesus, and sometimes as a madman,—so unintelligible to them are the objects and pleasures of travelling.

KARL BAEDECKER
*PALESTINE AND SYRIA: HANDBOOK FOR TRAVELLERS* (1906)

———

The lady tourist will ever be, to her sex at large, but as a meteoric flash amidst the hosts of fixed stars that stud the skies.

MABLE SHARMAN CRAWFORD (c. 1830–1860)
"THROUGH ALGERIA," *MAIDEN VOYAGES* (1993)

———

It is a magic of a different way of life.

RUPERT BROOKE
*LETTER FROM AMERICA* (1916)

My aunt had obviously spent many years abroad and this had affected her character as well as her morality.

GRAHAM GREENE
*TRAVELS WITH MY AUNT* (1969)

Life abroad is worse than exile to Siberia.

FYODOR DOSTOEVSKY (1821–1881)

Fake European standards have ruined you. You drink yourself to death. You become obsessed by sex. You spend all your time talking, not working. You hang around cafés.

ERNEST HEMINGWAY
*THE SUN ALSO RISES* (1926)

However much you may fight against it, if you live abroad where there are other expatriates, you become part of what is know as the Foreign Community.

CHRIS STEWART
*DRIVING OVER LEMONS* (1999)

———•••••———

What strikes me the most upon the whole is, the difference of manners between them and us, from the greatest object to the least.

HORACE WALPOLE, LETTER TO JOHN CHUTE, 1765
*THE LETTERS OF HORACE WALPOLE* (1891)

———•••••———

Apart from the fact that they prostitute their daughters, the Lydian way is not unlike our own.

HERODOTUS (c. 484–425 B.C.)

To travel is to discover that everyone is wrong about other countries.

ALDOUS HUXLEY (1894–1963)

I went around the world last year and you want to know something? It hates each other.

EDWARD J. MANNIX

In their view they were travelling to find themselves, rather as if oneself was a missing cufflink or earring that had rolled under the bed.

MARTHA GELLHORN
*TRAVELS WITH MYSELF AND ANOTHER* (1978)

I was quite taken out of myself and vowed a vow there to go to Rome on Pilgrimage and see all of Europe which the Christian Faith has saved.

HILAIRE BELLOC
*THE PATH TO ROME* (1902)

In the middle ages people were tourists because of their religion, whereas now they are tourists because tourism is their religion.

ROBERT RUNCIE, ARCHBISHOP OF CANTERBURY (1921– )

A modern airport is based on the assumption that everyone's from somewhere else.

PICO IYER
*GLOBAL SOUL* (2000)

In the railroads, some people read clearly printed departure signs and then proceed to ask several times what they say. On airplanes, they demand things they know they cannot have. In their cars, they load up, drive away and then suddenly realize they don't know where they're going.

LUCINDA FRANKS
"THOUSANDS INEPTLY GET AWAY FROM IT ALL," *NEW YORK TIMES*
30 AUGUST 1975

You visit sixteen countries in seventeen days but you fly real low over eight others.

JAMES A. MICHENER
*THE DRIFTERS* (1971)

The tourist who moves about to see and hear and open himself to all the influences of the places which condense centuries of human greatness is only a man in search of excellence.

MAX LERNER (1902– )

I sometimes think that Thomas Cook should be numbered among the secular saints. He took travel from the privileged and gave it to the people.

ROBERT RUNCIE, ARCHBISHOP OF CANTERBURY (1921– )

On Saturday, June 8, 1867, the steamship *Quaker City* left New York harbor. On board was a group of Americans making the world's first package tour. Also on board was Mark Twain making the world's first fun of package tourism.

P. J. O'ROARKE
*HOLIDAYS IN HELL* (1988)

I remember when to be a "Cook's tourist" was a thing to be ashamed of, and when everybody felt privileged to make fun of Cook's "personally conducted" gangs of economical provincials.

MARK TWAIN
"LETTERS TO SATAN" (1923)

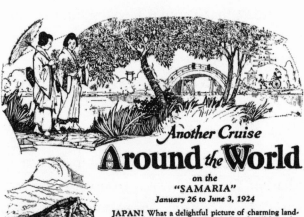

As a member of an escorted tour you don't even have to know the Matterhorn isn't a tuba.

TEMPLE FIELDING
*FIELDING'S GUIDE TO EUROPE* (1963)

———

The tourist travels in his own atmosphere like a snail in his shell and stands, as it were, on his own perambulating doorstep to look at the continents of the world.

FREYA STARK
*BAGHDAD SKETCHES* (1932)

———

At Opryland, the outdoors is indoors, and that, I realized with a shiver, is precisely the way many millions of people would have the whole world if it were possible.

BILL BRYSON
*I'M A STRANGER HERE MYSELF* (1999)

You perceive I generalize with intrepidity from single instances. It is the tourist's custom.

MARK TWAIN (1835–1910)

————

I once traveled with a party of New Yorkers *en route* for California. They were perfectly ignorant of everything relating to this kind of campaigning, and had overloaded their waggons with almost everything except the very articles most important and necessary; the consequence was, that they exhausted their teams, and were obliged to throw away the greater part of their loading. They soon learned that Champagne, East India sweetmeats, olives, etc., etc., were not the most useful articles for a prairie tour.

CAPTAIN R. B. MARCY
*THE PRAIRIE AND OVERLAND TRAVELER* (1860)

English travelers often impose considerable trouble by ordering things almost unknown in German usage, and are apt to become involved in disputes owing to their ignorance of the language.

KARL BAEDECKER
*THE EASTERN ALPS: HANDBOOK FOR TRAVELLERS* (1883)

You will find that your attempt to communicate in a foreign language will please the people you meet in that country, especially if you remember to use "Pardon me," "Please," "Thank you," and so on.

CHARLES BERLITZ
*PASSPORT TO THE WORLD* (1991)

Without a knowledge of languages you feel as if you don't have a passport.

Anton Chekhov (1860–1904)

He that traveleth into a country before he hath some entrance into the language, goeth to school, and not to travel.

> SIR FRANCIS BACON
> "OF TRAVEL" (1597)

Into the face of the young man who sat on the terrace of the Hôtel Magnifique at Cannes there had crept a look of furtive shame, the shifty, hangdog look which announces that an Englishman is about to talk French.

> P. G. WODEHOUSE
> *THE LUCK OF THE BODKINS* (1935)

"*!Wilkommen.* Welcome. *Bienvenida!*" I was afraid he was about to launch into *Cabaret.*

> SARA WHEELER
> *TRAVELS IN A THIN COUNTRY* (1999)

The American arrives in Paris with a few French phrases he has culled from a conversational guide or picked up from a friend who owns a beret.

FRED ALLEN, INTRODUCTION TO ART BUCHWALD'S
*PARIS AFTER DARK* (1954)

In Paris they simply stared when I spoke to them in French; I never did succeed in making those idiots understand their language.

MARK TWAIN (1835–1910)

No man should travel until he has learned the language of the country he visits. Otherwise he voluntarily makes himself a great baby—so helpless and so ridiculous.

RALPH WALDO EMERSON
*JOURNALS* (1833)

*Tant pis* and *tant mieux,* being two of the great hinges in French conversation, a stranger would do well to set himself right in the use of them before he gets to Paris.

LAURENCE STERNE
*A SENTIMENTAL JOURNEY THROUGH FRANCE AND ITALY* (1768)

As soon as I pass through customs at Gatwick, *lovely* begins to pop unbidden from my mouth.

SUSAN ALLEN TOTH
*ENGLAND FOR ALL SEASONS* (1997)

The important thing about travel in foreign lands is that it breaks the speech habits and makes you blab less . . .

PAUL GOODMAN (1911–1972)

Hearing Mass is the ceremony I most favor during my travels. Church is the only place where someone speaks to me . . . and I do not have to answer back.

CHARLES DE GAULLE
*NEWSWEEK* 1 OCTOBER 1962

These are the people that make life a burden to the tourist. Their tongues are never still. They talk forever and ever. Inspiration itself could hardly comprehend them.

MARK TWAIN, CRITICIZING TOUR GUIDES
*INNOCENTS ABROAD* (1869)

By expatriating himself, by living in Paris, Capri or the South of France, the artist can break the puritan shackles, drink, live freely and be wholly creative.

MALCOLM COWLEY
*EXILE'S RETURN* (1934)

I went to Asia, basically, to draw people.

> JOHN GROTH
> *STUDIO ASIA* (1952)

---

I realized that my drawing had created a sensation, but I did not let this disturb me and went calmly on with my work.

> JOHANN WOLFGANG VON GOETHE IN 1786
> *ITALIAN JOURNEY* (1961)

---

There followed a larger crowd; the tourists that always settle around painters.

> V. S. PRITCHETT
> *AT HOME AND ABROAD* (1989)

---

We staid two hours, rode back through the charming picture, wished for a painter, wished to be poets!

> HORACE WALPOLE, LETTER TO RICHARD WEST, 1739
> *THE LETTERS OF HORACE WALPOLE* (1891)

Everything is going to be different; life is never going to be the same again after your passport has been stamped.

GRAHAM GREENE
*ANOTHER MEXICO* (1939)

Travel is freedom. It's recess, and we need it.

RICK STEVES
*EUROPE THROUGH THE BACK DOOR* (1998)

Travel, as always, was the perfect solution for those who wanted to be free of grown-ups and yet not to grow up themselves.

IAN LITTLEWOOD
*SULTRY CLIMATES* (2001)

Travel, in the younger sort, is a part of education; in the elder, a part of experience.

SIR FRANCIS BACON
"OF TRAVEL" (1597)

Fish and visitors smell in three days.

BENJAMIN FRANKLIN
POOR RICHARD'S ALMANACK (1736)

It is equally offensive to speed a guest who would like to stay and to detain one who is anxious to leave.

HOMER
THE ODYSSEY (c. 700 B.C.)

I cannot rest from travel . . .

> ALFRED, LORD TENNYSON
> "Ulysses" (1842)

———•••••———

Who are the great travelers? They are curious, contented, self-sufficient people who are not afraid of the past. They are not hiding in travel; they are seeking.

> PAUL THEROUX
> *FRESH AIR FIEND* (2000)

———•••••———

They change their climate, not their soul, who rush across the sea.

> HORACE (65–8 B.C.)

If an ass goes traveling he will not come home a horse.

THOMAS FULLER,
*GNOMOLOGIA* (1732)

# 6

# Coming Home

BRING BACK THE WORLD

Most travel is really a 360-degree affair. You leave, do some things, see some things, and come back home. After a week or a month away, most of us look forward to returning to that which is familiar. That's also why vacations are sufficient for most of us, and why it is called a "vacation" and not a "move." We don't say "I moved to Italy for fourteen days," or "I've moved to the Caribbean for a week." We say, "I was on vacation." I vacated my regular life for a given time and now I'm back.

And returning home does have its rewards. One reason we yearn to get home is so that we can regale our friends and family with our stories of the exotic, unfamiliar places we've seen. There's no point in bragging to a man on the street in Nice that you've been to the French Riviera; he knows, he lives there, he's not impressed! Boasting to your relatives from Weehawken, New Jersey, on the other hand—whom you know have never left the state—is more satisfying. (Just ignore their glassy-eyed stares after you bring out the third photo album.)

Another great thing about being home? You get to plan your next vacation.

Every trip has to end.

CHARLES KURALT
*A LIFE ON THE ROAD* (1990)

Travel is glamorous only in retrospect.

PAUL THEROUX (1941– )

Travel is ninety percent anticipation and ten percent recollection.

EDWARD STREETER (1891–1976)

All travel is about return as well as departure.

MARY MORRIS
*MAIDEN VOYAGES* (1993)

. . . wondering how any journey can match the daydreams that precede it, or the extravagant memories that follow.

THURSTON CLARKE
*EQUATOR* (1988)

The time to enjoy a European tour is about three weeks after you unpack.

GEORGE ADE (1866–1944)

Most travel is best of all in the anticipation or the remembering; the reality has more to do with losing your luggage.

REGINA NADELSON

I have a trunk containing continents.

BERYL MARKHAM (1902–1956)

Well, don't worry about it . . . it was just a travel dream.

ANNE TYLER
*THE ACCIDENTAL TOURIST* (1985)

The alternative to a vacation is to stay at home and tip every third person you see.

ANONYMOUS

Most people know the feeling. You've been away someplace, had a great time. You get home and before you can even unpack your souvenirs, dreary old problems surface, dreary new problems crowd in.

ANDY LOGAN
*THE NEW YORKER* 9 APRIL 1984

Anyone who's ever been on a group tour almost always returns home with stomach-churning tales of their obnoxious fellow travelers, of people who actually say, "No Bruno, today's Tuesday, so this has to be Auschwitz!"

CRAIG NELSON
*LET'S GET LOST* (1999)

A journey is best measured in friends rather than miles.

TIM CAHILL
*ROAD FEVER* (1991)

Spirit of the place! It is for this we travel, to surprise its subtlety; and where it is a strong and dominant angel, that place, seen once, abides entire in the memory with all its own accidents, its habits, its breath, its name.

ALICE MEYNALL (1847–1922)

There are places I have been which are lost to me.

FRANCES MAYES
*UNDER THE TUSCAN SUN* (1997)

———————

I have a picture of the Pont Neuf on a wall in my apartment, but I know that Paris is really on the closet shelf, in the box next to the sleeping bag, with the rest of [my] diaries.

THOMAS MALLON
*NEW YORK TIMES* 21 JUNE 1985

———————

Reading my notes of the trip—images, bits of conversation, ideas—I hunted a structure in the event, but randomness was the rule.

WILLIAM LEAST HEAT-MOON
*BLUE HIGHWAYS* (1982)

My thoughts brushed over the years and miles of my journey, tracing the fear as it has waxed and waned along the way, trying to hold it all together and reassure myself that there really had been a beginning. Without a beginning how could there be an end?

TED SIMON
*JUPITER'S TRAVELS* (1979)

Traveling is not just seeing the new; it is also leaving behind. Not just opening doors; also closing them behind you, never to return. But the place you have left forever is always there for you to see whenever you shut your eyes.

JAN MYRDAL
*THE SILK ROAD* (1980)

God willing, I'll be back.

TONY COHAN
*ON MEXICAN TIME* (2000)

So for the next month or two I shall be reliving my journey in Guiana and Brazil. Not that it has ever been out of my memory.

EVELYN WAUGH
*WHEN THE GOING WAS GOOD* (1934)

Bathed in the last dopamine rays of sun, we've reached that moment in the course of every road trip when exhaustion and discombobulation spill into a kind of ecstasy.

MICHAEL PATERNITI
*DRIVING MR. ALBERT* (2000)

Travel is the most private of pleasures. There is no greater bore than the travel bore. We do not in the least want to hear what he has seen in Hong Kong.

VITA SACKVILLE-WEST,
*PASSENGER TO TEHERAN* (1926)

Some were old and alone, some weird and friendless, some had friends but were in danger of losing them if they subjected them to another illustrated account of their last vacation, some were simply incorrigible show-offs. What they all had in common was that each of them had been somewhere and wanted to tell someone about it.

TOM ROBBINS
*HALF ASLEEP IN FROG PAJAMAS* (1994)

A traveler has a right to relate and embellish his adventures as he pleases, and it is very impolite to refuse that deference and applause they deserve.

RUDOLF ERICH RASPE
*TRAVELS OF BARON MÜNCHAUSEN* (1786)

I have perused several books of travels with great delight in my younger days; but having since gone over most parts of the globe, and been able to contradict many fabulous accounts from my own observation, it has given me a great disgust against this part of reading, and some indignation to see the credulity of mankind so impudently abused.

JONATHAN SWIFT
*GULLIVER'S TRAVELS* (1726)

Old men and far travelers may lie with authority.

ANONYMOUS

For *the kingdom of heaven* is as a man traveling into a far country.

MATTHEW 25:14

The only aspect of our travels that is guaranteed to hold an audience is disaster.

MARTHA GELLHORN
*TRAVELS WITH MYSELF AND ANOTHER* (1978)

I think of this as the English way of traveling—the ability to make one good story stand for a vast, messy ordeal.

PAUL THEROUX
*FRESH AIR FIEND* (2000)

For me, exploration was a personal venture. I did not go to the Arabian desert to collect plants or make a map; such things were incidental. At heart I knew that to write or even talk of my travels was to tarnish the achievement.

WILFRED THESINGER
*ARABIAN SANDS* (1959)

I realized that many of the most important changes in my life had come about because of my travel experiences.

MICHAEL CRICHTON
*TRAVELS* (1988)

Traveling is like gambling: it is always connected with winning and losing, and generally where it is least expected we receive, more or less than what we hoped for.

JOHANN WOLFGANG VON GOETHE (1749–1832)

Mosquitoes—Frogs—Beastly. Glad to see the end of this stupid tramp. Feel rather seedy.

JOSEPH CONRAD
*THE CONGO DIARY* (1902)

I wasn't particularly equipped for this trip.

> JOE KANE
> *RUNNING THE AMAZON* (1989)

Of course world travel isn't as good as it seems, it's only after you've come back from all the heat and horror that you forget to get bugged and remember the weird scenes you saw.

> JACK KEROUAC
> "BIG TRIP TO EUROPE," *LONESOME TRAVELER* (1960)

When a traveller returneth home, let him not leave the countries where he hath travelled behind him . . .

> SIR FRANCIS BACON
> "ON TRAVEL" (1597)

I hated ending the journey this way, but in another sense I didn't mind it at all.

EDDY L. HARRIS, ON HITCHING A RIDE IN ANOTHER BOAT FOR THE
LAST MILE OF HIS RIDE DOWN THE RIVER
*MISSISSIPPI SOLO* (1988)

A hundred miles of traveling on water, and I was ready for a rest.

PETER JENKINS
*ALONG THE EDGE OF AMERICA* (1995)

It makes me sheepish to report that when Richard and I brought the children back to the United States, the dulcet tones of "Be It Ever So Humble" were drowned out by the mundane question of plumbing.

RUTH McKENNEY
*FAR, FAR FROM HOME* (1952)

Knowledge of [another] culture should sharpen our ability to scrutinize more steadily, to appreciate more lovingly, our own.

MARGARET MEAD
*COMING OF AGE IN SAMOA* (1928)

We grow more confident at the price of knowing the world, and therefore ourselves.

JOE KANE
*RUNNING THE AMAZON* (1989)

We wallowed in the convenience of America, in the efficiency and the extraordinary variety of choice, and we practiced native customs.

PETER MAYLE
*ENCORE PROVENCE* (1999)

I was glad to get home—immeasurably glad; so glad, in fact, that it did not seem possible that anything could ever get me out of the country again.

MARK TWAIN
*A TRAMP ABROAD* (1880)

A–roving, a–roving,
Since roving's been my ru–i–in,
I'll go no more a–roving
With you fair maid!

ANONYMOUS SHANDY

Journeys end in lovers meeting.

WILLIAM SHAKESPEARE (1564–1616)

# 7

# The Armchair Traveler

Some people travel vicariously through other people's adventures. They pore over travel magazines and the travel section of the Sunday newspaper, tagging along from place to place with travel writers, sharing their journeys with them. Each week they revel in the details of a new destination: last week a beach, this week a city, next week the mountains. In winter they ski in Europe and in summer they fish in Canada. No matter their ages or their athletic abilities, they raft the mighty rivers of South America, surf the rolling waves off Hawaii, and climb the steepest peaks of the Himalayas. They barter with crafty merchants in old Arabic cities and barge with well-heeled travelers on French canals. Ask them about any city, anywhere, and they can tell you in which five-star hotel or two-star bed-and-breakfast they would stay. They are intimate with the maître d'hôtel of the most fashionable restaurant in Paris and with the padrone of the most rustic inn in Calabria. Which sight to see? How to avoid tourist traps? They can always tell you. They know the best season to travel to a given destination and what to wear when they get there. (*They* would never be conspicuous Americans.) They face no delays, never lose their luggage or brangle with customs agents, and always speak the native language. And best of all, no matter where they go, they get to travel in their own first-class seats!

What child has not traveled by spinning a globe?

THURSTON CLARKE
*EQUATOR* (1988)

What self-respecting armchair traveler stuck too long in home port with a dyspeptic boss and absently spinning a globe, hasn't done a mental 180, imagining jamming a pencil through the globe and drifting off to wherever the pencil comes out, far, far, away?

MIKE TIDWELL
*IN THE MOUNTAINS OF HEAVEN* (2000)

I'm a gypsy in spirit only.... I travel in gardens and bedrooms, basements and attics, around corners, through doorways and windows, along sidewalks, up stairs, over carpets, down drainpipes, in the sky, with friends, lovers, children and heroes; perceived, remembered, imagined, distorted and clarified.

TOM ROBBINS
*ANOTHER ROADSIDE ATTRACTION* (1972)

I was game for distraction—but not if I had to travel 2500 miles for it.

SARA WHEELER
*TRAVELS IN A THIN COUNTRY* (1999)

———•·••·•———

I wouldn't mind seeing China if I could come back the same day.

PHILIP LARKIN
*NEW YORK TIMES* 3 DECEMBER 1985

———•·••·•———

He decided if he couldn't travel physically, he would travel mentally.

GRAHAM GREENE
*TRAVELS WITH MY AUNT* (1969)

———•·••·•———

Had he traveled? It was likely, for no one seemed to know the world more familiarly; there was no spot so secluded that he did not appear to have an intimate acquaintance with it. He often corrected, with a few clear words, the thousand conjectures advanced by members of the club as to lost and unheard-of travelers, pointing out the true probabilities, and seeming as if gifted with a sort of second sight, so often did events justify his predictions. He must have traveled everywhere, at least in the spirit.

JULES VERNE
*AROUND THE WORLD IN EIGHTY DAYS* (1873)

I wouldn't think of going into any out-of-the-way place without familiarizing myself, through reading, with the human inhabitants and ecosystems of that particular region.

JOHN WALDEN
*JUNGLE TRAVEL AND SURVIVAL* (2001)

We pored over atlases.

BRUCE CHATWIN
*IN PATAGONIA* (1977)

About the time my job started to go bad a few years ago, I began collecting maps and considering places I would rather be.

ROBERT ALDEN RUBIN
*ON THE BEATEN TRACK* (2000)

Timbuktu. The end of everybody's road. The capital of Nowhere. Geography's perennial avant-garde and the armchair traveler's inevitable cul-de-sac.

TOM ROBBINS
*HALF ASLEEP IN FROG PAJAMAS* (1994)

"And Tibet," he said, "there's always Tibet . . ."

BRUCE CHATWIN
*WHAT AM I DOING HERE* (1989)

In the circumstances anyone who had actually spent a few weeks in Abyssinia itself, and had read the dozen or so books which constituted the entire English bibliography of the subject, might claim to be an expert.

EVELYN WAUGH, ON HOW HE GOT HIMSELF HIRED AS A WAR
CORRESPONDENT TO ETHIOPIA
*WAUGH IN ABYSSINIA* (1935)

Before long I found myself committed—in the capacity of special correspondent to *The Times*—to a venture for which Rider Haggard might have written the plot and Conrad designed the scenery.

PETER FLEMING, ON HOW HE FINANCED HIS JOURNEY THROUGH THE
INTERIOR OF BRAZIL
*BRAZILIAN ADVENTURE* (1933)

The Best Time to Visit

SOUTH AMERICA!

Thanks to newspapers, I have made a four-hour visit to Afghanistan, have seen the Taj Mahal by moonlight, breakfasted at dawn on lamb and couscous while sitting by the marble pool of a Moorish palace in Morocco and once picked up a persistent family of fleas in the Balkans.

RUSSELL BAKER (1925– )

As a nation, we are the children of those who tried to solve old problems with a new place, and that may be why the first writing about America comes from explorers and why other travelers' accounts have flourished for half a millennium.

WILLIAM LEAST HEAT-MOON
BLUE HIGHWAYS (1982)

Life, as the most ancient of all metaphors insists, is a journey; and the travel book, in its deceptive simulation of the journey's fits and starts, rehearses life's own fragmentation.

More even than a novel, it embraces the contingency of things.

JONATHAN RABAN

More even than a novel, it embraces the contingency of things.

Yet travel books remain the weak sisters of literature, feeble both in bookstores and in most critics' esteem.

EDWARD HOAGLAND
*THE TUGMAN'S PASSAGE* (1982)

Yet I was loath to let the whole thing go unrecorded. Was it for this that I had gone footsore, cold, hot, wet, hungry? climbed up, and scrambled down? covered all those miles? looked at all those goats?

VITA SACKVILLE-WEST, ON HER REASON FOR WRITING A BOOK
ABOUT HER TRAVELS IN PERSIA
*TWELVE DAYS* (1928)

I could heartily wish a law was enacted, that every traveller, before he were permitted to publish his voyages, should be obliged to make oath before the Lord High Chancellor, that all he intended to print was absolutely true to the best of his knowledge; for then the world would no longer be deceived, as it usually is, while some writers, to make their works pass the better upon the public, impose the grossest falsities on the unwary reader.

JONATHAN SWIFT
*GULLIVER'S TRAVELS* (1726)

And why do the worst journeys make the best books?

LARRY MCMURTRY
*ROADS* (2000)

The rest of the trip was monotonous.

TIZIANO TENZANI
*A FORTUNE TELLER TOLD ME* (1997)

All that is the idle fancy of frivolous travellers.

> FYODOR DOSTOEVSKY
> "THE CROCODILE" (1865)

—————

Emperors and kings, dukes and marquises, counts, knights, and townsfolk, and all people who wish to know the various races of men and the peculiarities of the various regions of the world, take this book and have it read to you.

> MARCO POLO
> *THE TRAVELS OF MARCO POLO* (c. 1298)

—————

Many of the best travel writers are odd ducks.

> EDWARD HOAGLAND
> *THE TUGMAN'S PASSAGE* (1982)

—————

Travel is not compulsory. Great minds have been fostered entirely by staying close to home. Moses never got further than the Promised Land. Da Vinci and Beethoven never left Europe. Shakespeare hardly went anywhere at all—certainly not to Elsinore or the coast of Bohemia.

JAN MORRIS (JAMES MORRIS)
"IT'S OK TO STAY AT HOME," *NEW YORK TIMES* 30 AUGUST 1985

Allow me to remind you in a few words of how certain ardent minds set off on imaginary journeys and claimed to have discovered the secrets of our satellite.

JULES VERNE
*FROM THE EARTH TO THE MOON* (1865)

It's all very well, to set off on a train with no money telling yourself you're really quite a brave and adventurous person . . . but when you actually arrive at the other end with no one to meet you and nowhere to go . . . it suddenly seems much more attractive to be home . . . reading about camels.

ROBYN DAVIDSON
*TRACKS* (1980)

The dear repose for limbs with travel tired,
But then begins a journey in my head
To work my mind, when body's works expired.

> SIR FRANCIS BACON
> *MARGUERITE*, SONNET NO. 27

Whoever claimed that travel is merely home in motion was traveling in an armchair—or else engaged in travel (as Samuel Butler once put it) too easy to deserve the name.

> KEATH FRASER
> *BAD TRIPS* (1991)

When the wind is blowing and the sleet or rain is driving against the dark windows, I love to sit by the fire, thinking of what I have read in books of voyage and travel.

> CHARLES DICKENS (1812–1870)

Come and step on my carpet! We're going to the South Seas to the islands you've read about, sitting before the fire at night time.

HECTOR MACQUARRIE
*TAHITI DAYS* (1920)

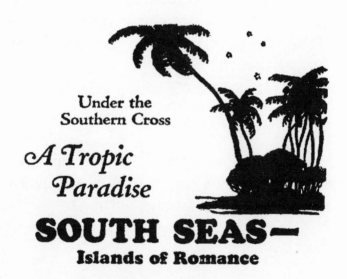

The wise traveller travels only in imagination. . . . Those are the best journeys, the journeys that you take at your own fireside, for then you lose none of your illusions.

W. SOMERSET MAUGHAM
"HONOLULU," *THE TREMBLING OF A LEAF* (1921)

The armchair explorer, snug in his living room, does not have to endure the heat, cold, mud, dust, insects, fevers, and occasional dangers faced by the foolish handful who are compelled to journey to the few remote and wild places remaining on this overcrowded and over-charted planet.

PHILIP CAPUTO, FOREWORD TO *GREATER NOWHERES*
BY DAVE FINKELSTEIN AND JACK LONDON (1988)

He that travels in theory has no inconveniences; he has shade and sunshine at his disposal, and wherever he alights finds tables of plenty and looks of gaiety.

SAMUEL JOHNSON (1709–1784)

While armchair travelers dream of going places, traveling armchairs dream of staying put.

ANNE TYLER
*THE ACCIDENTAL TOURIST* (1985)

# Who's Who

**Adams, Douglas** (1952–2001), science-fiction humorist who sought to answer the ultimate question of life, the universe, and everything.

**Adams, Philip Andrew,** Australian writer.

**Ade, George** (1866–1944), American anti-imperialist writer of satirical fables.

**Allen, Fred** (1894–1956), vaudevillian and radio comedian.

**Amis, Martin** (1949– ), British novelist and essayist, son of author Kingsley Amis.

**Arbus, Diane** (1923–1971), American photographer known for haunting black-and-white portraits.

**Aron, Jean Paul,** French essayist.

**Austen, Jane** (1775–1817), British novelist known for witty social satire and quiet romantic comedy.

**Bacon, Sir Francis** (1561–1625), Elizabethan essayist, poet, and writer.

**Baedecker, Karl,** publisher of numerous travel guides that were widely read during the late 19th and early 20th centuries.

**Baker, Russell** (1925– ), former *New York Times* columnist, armchair host of "Masterpiece Theatre," and Pulitzer Prize–winning author.

**Ballard, Sarah,** sportswriter.

**Baltimore, George Calvert, 1st Baron** (c. 1580–1632), colonialist and founder of Maryland.

**Barich, Bill,** novelist, short-story writer, and essayist on such diverse subjects as fly fishing, boxing, and Italian culture.

**Barry, Dave** (1947– ), syndicated humor columnist and Pulitzer Prize winner.

**Beecham, Sir Thomas** (1879–1961), English symphony conductor.

**Belmont, Eleanor Robson** (1879–1979), Anglo-American actor, writer, and nurse.

**Belloc, Hilaire** (1870–1953), English writer, editor, historian, and author of caustically humorous verse for children.

**Berlitz, Charles** (1914– ), gifted linguist and author of more than 150 language-instruction books; grandson of the founder of the famous Berlitz Schools.

**Berman, Shelley** (1926– ), American comedian.

**Bion,** Greek poet who lived in the 1st or 2nd century.

**Bird, Isabella** (1831–1904), British world traveler who circled the globe three times and was the first woman elected to the Royal Geographic Society.

**Bombeck, Erma** (1927–1996), American columnist and humorist.

**Brooke, Rupert** (1887–1915), English poet whose untimely death during World War I made him a symbol of all the gifted youth killed in that war.

**Bryson, Bill,** travel writer, best known for his hilarious observations on the absurdities of his fellow human beings.

**Bunyan, John** (1628–88), English writer and Puritan minister; author of religious allegories.

**Burnby, Colonel Fred,** British officer of the Royal House Guards, master of many languages, balloonist, and travel writer.

**Burton, Sir Richard** (1821–1890), one of the most famous mid-19th century European explorers of Africa.

**Cahill, Tim,** acclaimed outdoor writer, world traveler, and misadventurer.

**Cain, James M.** (1892–1977), master of the hard-boiled detective genre.

**Calvino, Italo** (1923–1985), whimsical Italian journalist, short-story writer, and novelist.

**Caputo, Philip** (1941– ), contemporary American author and journalist.

**Carty, Dave,** Montana-based essay writer.

**Charles** (1948– ), Prince of Wales and heir apparent to the throne of the United Kingdom of Great Britain and Northern Ireland.

**Chateaubriand, François Auguste René, Vicomte de** (1768–1848), French writer, statesman, and pioneer of the Romantic Movement.

**Chatwin, Bruce** (1940–1989), traveler, adventurer, and writer.

**Chaucer, Geoffrey** (c. 1340–1400), English poet and master storyteller.

**Chekhov, Anton** (1860–1904), Russian author and playwright.

**Cheever, John** (1912–1982), American writer, best known for his short stories dealing with the ironies of suburban middle-class life.

**Christie, Dame Agatha** (1890–1976), English novelist and prolific writer of mystery stories, creator of memorable detectives Hercule Poirot and Miss Marple.

**Clarke, Thurston,** contemporary American travel writer.

**Cohan, Tony,** American writer who spent 15 years in Mexico.

**Collis, Louise,** biographer of the medieval diarist Margery Kempe.

**Confucius** (c. 551–479 B.C.), Chinese sage.

**Conrad, Joseph** (1857–1924), Polish-born Jósef Teodor Konrad, who went on to become a noted modern English writer.

**Cooper, James Fenimore** (1789–1851), New Jersey-born novelist, social critic, and travel writer.

**Cowley, Malcolm** (1898–1989), editor, literary critic, and social historian who chronicled the lives of the Lost Generation.

**Crawford, Mable Sharman** (c. 1830–1860), 19th-century traveler to North Africa.

**Crichton, Michael** (1942– ), American novelist and screenwriter, known for his blockbuster science-fiction thrillers.

**Crosse, William Henry, M.D.,** turn-of-the-century writer of medical hints.

**Cunliffe, Tom** (1947– ), British writer and columnist who, with his wife, journeyed across America on a Harley Davidson.

**Dahlberg, Edward** (1900–1977), American novelist, critic, and essayist.

**David-Néel, Alexandra** (1868–1969), indefatigable French writer and adventurer who traveled extensively through the Far East and Central Asia.

**Davidson, Robyn** (1950– ), intrepid Australian travel writer.

**Debord, Guy** (1931– ), one of the founders of the situationist movement of the 1960s; attained notoriety during the Paris street revolution of 1968.

**Defoe, Daniel** (1660?–1731), English adventure novelist, journalist, and pamphleteer.

**de Gaulle, Charles** (1890–1970), French general and statesman; first president of the Fifth Republic.

**Dickens, Charles** (1812–1870), widely popular and prodigiously productive Victorian-era English author.

**Dickens, Monica,** great-granddaughter of Charles Dickens.

**Dostoevsky, Fyodor** (1821–1881), influential novelist, essayist, and journalist who wrote fevered tales of everyday Russian life.

**Doughty, Charles Montagu,** grand, but often opaque writer and traveler of the late 19th century.

**Douglas-Home, Robin** (1932–1968), British aristocrat.

**Doyle, Sir Arthur Conan** (1859–1930), British creator of Sherlock Holmes, the best-known detective in literature.

**Dreiser, Theodore** (1871–1945), American novelist, a pioneer of naturalism in literature.

**Durrell, Lawrence** (1912–1990), English novelist and diplomat; born in India.

**Edwards, Amelia Blanford** (1831–1892), journalist, suffragist, novelist, and Egyptologist, known for her travelers' tales.

**Emerson, Ralph Waldo** (1803–1882), American transcendentalist essayist and poet.

**Evans, Julian** (1955– ), contemporary literary critic and traveler.

**Fermor, Patrick Leigh** (1915– ), Englishman who according to Jan Morris is "beyond cavil the greatest of living travel writers."

**Fielding, Temple** (1913– ), author of a famous series of guides to European travel.

**Fleming, Peter,** self-deprecating, but always entertaining, 20th-century travel writer.

**Fraser, John Foster,** early-20th-century traveler and writer.

**Fraser, Keath** (1944– ), Canadian novelist and travel writer.

**Franklin, Benjamin** (1706–1790), inventor, philosopher, publisher, statesman, and traveler.

**Franks, Lucinda,** Pulitzer Prize–winning journalist.

**Frayn, Michael** (1933– ), English dramatist, columnist, reporter, and translator.

**Friedrich, Otto** (d. 1995), historian, journalist, and adventurer.

**Fry, Christopher** (1907– ), British dramatist.

**Fuller, Thomas** (1608–1661), English clergyman, author, and noted wit.

**Fussell, Paul** (1924– ), American historian.

**Galton, Sir Francis** (1822–1911), British traveler and scientist, considered to be the founder of the science of eugenics.

**Gellhorn, Martha** (1908–1998), American journalist, novelist, and war correspondent during the Spanish Civil War and World War II; third wife of Ernest Hemingway.

**George V** (1865–1936), king of the United Kingdom of Great Britain and Northern Ireland, and emperor of India (1910–1936), known as the Sailor Prince.

**Geyer, Georgie Ann** (1935– ), contemporary travel writer and foreign correspondent.

**Goethe, Johann Wolfgang von,** (1749–1832), German poet, dramatist, novelist, and scientist.

**Golding, William** (1911–1993), English author and Nobel Prize winner.

**Goodman, Paul** (1911–1972), artist and social critic.

**Grahame, Kenneth** (1859–1932), author of fanciful prose, born in Edinburgh, Scotland.

**Greene, Graham** (1904–1991), English novelist, short-story writer, playwright, and journalist.

**Groth, John** (1908– ), prolific illustrator, war correspondent, first art director of *Esquire* magazine, and longtime instructor at the Art Students League of New York.

**Gunther, John** (1901–1970), American journalist and foreign correspondent.

**Halliburton, Richard** (1900–1939), intrepid British traveler and writer who climbed the Matterhorn, swam the Panama Canal and the Hellespont, and crossed the Himalayas (among other treks).

**Hanley, Gerald** (1916– ), rancher, war correspondent, major in British army, and novelist.

**Hardy, Thomas** (1840–1928), largely pessimistic English novelist and poet.

**Hare, Augustus J. C.,** English writer of late-19th-century travel guides.

**Harris, Eddy L.,** American travel writer.

**Haun, Catherine,** mid-19th-century American pioneer who journeyed from Iowa to California.

**Hawks, Tony,** British writer, performer, and radio host.

**Heat-Moon, William Least** (1934– ), American travel writer.

**Hemingway, Ernest** (1899–1961), terse American novelist and short-story writer.

**Henry, O.,** pseudonym of William Sydney Porter (1862– 1910), American short story writer, best known for his ironic plot twists and surprise endings.

**Heraclitus** (c. 535–475 B.C.), Greek philosopher.

**Herodotus** (484?–425 B.C.), Greek writer, known as the father of history.

**Herrera, Susana,** former Peace Corps volunteer, now teacher and writer.

**Hesse, Hermann** (1877–1962), German novelist who often wrote of the spiritual loneliness of the artist.

**Highwater, Jamake,** traveler who writes extensively on culture and history.

**Hilton, James** (1900–1954), English novelist and screenwriter.

**Hoagland, Edward,** professor, essayist, and nature writer.

**Homer** (c. 700 B.C.), early Greek poet of whom very little is known.

**Horace** (Quintus Horatius Flaccus) (65–8 B.C.), Latin lyric poet.

**Horwitz, Tony** (1958– ), staff writer for *The New Yorker*, former foreign correspondent, and Pulitzer Prize winner.

**Humphries, Mrs. C. E.,** turn-of-the-century British traveler.

**Hunt, Lindsay,** editor and travel journalist.

**Huxley, Aldous** (1894–1963), English novelist, essayist, critic, and poet.

**Huxley, Elspeth** (1907– ), African-raised writer of novels, memoirs, and biographies.

**Iyer, Pico,** eloquent and incisive postmodern travel writer and novelist.

**James, Henry** (1843–1916), expatriate American writer of psychologically complex novels.

**Jefferson, Thomas** (1743–1826), 3rd president of the United States (1801–1809), philosopher, educator, naturalist, politician, scientist, architect, inventor, musician, writer, and traveler.

**Jenkins, Peter,** Tennessee photographer and travel writer.

**Jerome, Jerome K.** (1859–1927), humorous English novelist.

**Johnson, Samuel** (1709–1784), English lexicographer, critic, and conversationalist.

**Johnston, H. H.,** late-19th-century writer of travel guides.

**Jones, Tristan** (1924–1995), Welsh sailor, adventurer, and writer.

**Kane, Elisha Kent, M.D.,** 19th-century traveler.

**Kane, Joe,** San Francisco-based writer.

**Kantor, MacKinlay** (1904–1977), Iowa-born novelist.

**Kaplan, Robert D.** (1952– ), contributing editor to *The Atlantic Monthly* and author of books on foreign affairs and travel.

**Karr, Mary,** professor of English Literature and writer of popular nonfiction.

**Keene, Carolyn,** pseudonym of Mildred Wirt and others who have ghostwritten the Nancy Drew mysteries.

**Keller, Helen Adams** (1880–1968), American author and well-traveled lecturer.

**Kennedy, Jacqueline Bouvier** (1929–1994), elegant and elusive First Lady.

**Kerouac, Jack** (1922–1967), American writer, poet, and restless wanderer of the Beat generation.

**Kesey, Ken** (1935– ), American counterculture author, creator of the Acid Test scene that defined the image of the 1960s' Hippies.

**Kinglake, A. W.,** 19th-century historian and travel writer.

**Kingsley, Mary** (1862–1900), British explorer of West and Central Africa, who was the first European to visit parts of Gabon.

**Kipling, Rudyard** (1865–1936), imperialistic British poet.

**Koning, Hans** (1921– ), Dutch-born American writer.

**Kundera, Milan** (1929– ), humorous, but pessimistic Czech novelist.

**Kuralt, Charles** (1934–1997), foreign correspondent and television reporter and producer who upon retiring took a year-long journey from one corner of the United States to the other.

**Lancaster, Sir Osbert** (1908– ), English art historian.

**Lansky, Doug,** travel columnist and regular contributor to NPR's "Savvy Traveler."

**Lao-Tzu** (c. 570–490 B.C.), Chinese philosopher, credited as the founder of Daoism.

**Larkin, Philip** (1922–85), subtle English poet adept at exposing the pretensions of English life.

**Lawrence, D. H.** (1885–1930), controversial English novelist and poet.

**Lee, Laurie** (1914–1998), English poet and novelist.

**Lerner, Max** (1902–1992), Russian-born columnist.

**Lillie, Beatrice** (Lady Peel) (1898–1989), droll British comedienne.

**Littlewood, Ian,** British professor and writer of literary companions to Paris and Venice.

**Logan, Andy,** American nonfiction writer.

**Loos, Anita** (1888–1981), witty screenwriter, playwright, and novelist of early Hollywood.

**Loomis, Susan Herrmann,** writer and cook; lives in France.

**Machado y Ruíz, Antonio** (1875–1939), Spanish poet and member of the literary movement known as the Generation of 1898.

**MacQuarrie, Hector,** 20th-century traveler and writer.

**Mallon, Thomas** (1951– ), American novelist, essayist, and critic.

**Mamet, David** (1947– ), contemporary American playwright.

**Mannix, Edward J.,** writer.

**Marcy, Captain R. B.,** 19th-century guide and traveler.

**Markham, Beryl** (1902–1956), Kenyan-bred aviator, who was the first woman pilot to fly solo east to west across the Atlantic.

**Marx, Groucho** (1895–1977), wisecracking American comedian known for his outrageous asides, who with his brothers, Harpo, Chico, Gummo, and Zeppo, formed the Marx Brothers.

**Matthiessen, Peter,** curious and incisive novelist, nature writer, and traveler.

**Maugham, W. Somerset** (1874–1965), English author noted for his ironic and detached style.

**Maxwell, Gavin** (1914–1969), writer of bleak, if lyrical, memoirs.

**Mayes, Frances,** Georgia-born poet and prolific food and travel writer who now lives in Italy.

**Mayle, Peter,** advertising executive-turned-writer, who's credited with "discovering Provence" in the 1980s.

**Mayle, Simon** (1961– ), offbeat Anglo-American travel writer.

**McKenney, Ruth** (1911– ), light-hearted novelist and short story writer.

**McMurtry, Larry** (1936– ), Texas author noted for his depictions of the American West.

**Mead, Margaret** (1901–1978), American anthropologist best known for her work in Samoa.

**Melville, Herman** (1819–1891), American novelist, obscure in his own day.

**Meynall, Alice Thompson** (1847–1922), English poet and essayist.

**Michener, James A.** (1907–1997), American writer known for his voluminously researched works.

**Montaigne, Michel Eyquem de** (1533–1592), insatiably curious humanist scholar and essayist.

**More, Sir Thomas** (1478–1535), English writer and statesman whose opposing religious stance against Henry VIII cost him his life.

**Morland, Miles,** British novelist and travel writer.

**Morris, Jan** (formerly James Morris) (1926– ), British historian, journalist, and travel writer.

**Morris, Mary,** Brooklyn-based writer and editor.

**Moryson, Fynes,** 17th-century English gentleman-traveler.

**Moyes, Patricia** (1923– ), British mystery writer whose mild-mannered Inspector Tibbet often visits exotic locales.

**Myrdal, Jan,** Swedish sociologist.

**Nadelson, Regina,** American writer.

**Naipaul, V. S.** (Vidiadhar Surajprasad) (1932– ), Britain-based post-colonialist novelist and essayist.

**Nelson, Craig,** American editor, agent, and writer of humorous travelogues.

**Neves, Sylvaine Rouy,** writer.

**Newby, Eric,** longtime traveler and author.

**Norwich, John Julius,** member of House of Lords, historian, and traveler.

**Nugent, Thomas,** 18th-century scholar, antiquarian, and writer of a guidebook to European travel for aristocratic Englishmen.

**O'Roarke, P. J.** (1947– ), best-selling author, editor, and satirist who writes for many diverse periodicals from *Car and Driver* and *Playboy* to *The New Republic* and *Rolling Stone.*

**Ozick, Cynthia** (1928– ), writer of essays and creator of densely metaphorical fiction.

**Palin, Michael** (1943– ), one of the founders of Monty Python, the innovative English comedy troupe, writer, actor, and imaginative traveler.

**Paterniti, Michael,** freelance writer-at-large who lives in Maine.

**Paul VI** (1897–1978), Italian-born Giovanni Batista Montini became pope in 1963 and traveled widely to extend the Vatican's influence.

**Pauly, David,** American journalist.

**Pelton, Robert Young,** author and adventurer whose work has taken him through the world's most remote and dangerous places.

**Perelman, S. J.** (1904–1979), archly satirical American humorist whose essays were *New Yorker* fixtures for many years.

**Polo, Marco** (1254–1324), Venetian traveler and author of the account of his journeys and experiences in China.

**Porter, Ann E.,** 19th-century American writer.

**Pritchett, Sir V. S.** (1900–1997), gently ironic British writer.

**Raban, Jonathan,** Seattle-based travel writer.

**Raspe, Rudolf Erich** (1737–1794), librarian who chronicled the life of adventurer Karl Friedrich Hieronymus Baron von Münchhausen.

**Ritz, Charles,** scion of the Ritz family of world-class hotel fame.

**Robbins, Tom** (1936– ), offbeat and inventive American novelist.

**Robson, Eric,** British reporter and freelance writer.

**Rubin, Robert Alden,** former teacher, now journalist and senior editor of the Appalachian Trail Conference.

**Rudd, Lydia Allen,** 19th-century American pioneer diarist.

**Runcie, Robert** (1921– ), 102nd Archbishop of Canterbury from 1980 to 1991, known for his travels through Africa on behalf of the Anglican ministry.

**Russell, John,** writer.

**Sackville-West, Vita** (1892–1962), English poet, novelist, and traveler; one of the Bloomsbury group.

**Saint-Exupéry, Antoine Marie Roger de** (1900–1944), French writer, humanistic philosopher, and aviator.

**Sayers, Dorothy L.** (1893–1957), student of medieval literature and creator of the witty aristocratic detective Lord Peter Wimsey.

**Schultheis, Rob,** journalist and writer who makes his home in the Four Corners country of Colorado.

**Shakespeare, William** (1564–1616), the English playwright.

**Shaw, George Bernard** (1856–1950), Irish-born writer, dramatist, playwright, pamphleteer, music critic, theater critic, and letter writer.

**Sikorsky, Igor Ivanovich** (1889–1972), Russian-born American aeronautical engineer and manufacturer.

**Simenon, Georges,** principal pseudonym of Belgian-French Georges Sim (1903–1989), prolific writer of psychologically insightful novels and a series of detective fiction.

**Simon, Ted,** English journalist and travel writer who took a four-year trip around the world on the seat of a Triumph motorcycle.

**Sinclair, Iain,** British literary critic.

**Slocum, Captain Joshua,** traveler who set out at age 51 to circumnavigate the globe solo.

**Solzhenitsyn, Aleksandr Isayevich** (1918– ), Russian writer and Nobel laureate.

**de Staël, Madame** (Anne Louise Germaine, Baronne de Staël-Holstein) (1766–1817), French writer and intellectual.

**Stark, Dame Freya** (1893–1993), British traveler and writer of more than 30 travel books on life in the Middle East.

**Steel, Ronald,** American writer.

**Steinbeck, John** (1902–1968), American Nobel laureate.

**Sterne, Laurence** (1713–1768), English novelist and humorist.

**Stevens, Stuart,** contemporary travel writer.

**Stevenson, Robert Louis Balfour** (1850–1894), Scottish novelist, essayist, poet, and traveler.

**Steves, Rick,** travel guide writer and host of a Public television series *Travels in Europe with Rick Steves.*

**Stewart Chris** (1951– ), British travel writer living in Spain.

**Streeter, Edward** (1891–1976), American banker-turned-novelist.

**Swift, Jonathan** (1667–1745), English satirist of human folly.

**Tennyson, Alfred, 1st Baron Tennyson** (1809–1892), English poet of the Victorian Age.

**Tenzani, Tiziano,** U.S.-educated Far East correspondent for *Der Spiegel* who lived in Asia more than 30 years.

**Terán, Lisa St. Aubin de** (1953– ), novelist and poet who has written two memoirs of her years in Italy.

**Theroux, Paul** (1941– ), curmudgeonly American novelist, non-fiction author, and indefatigable traveler.

**Thesinger, Wilfred,** consummate 20th-century British traveler and writer.

**Thicknesse, Captain Philip,** 18th-century traveler and writer.

**Thompson, Brian,** Yorkshire novelist and playwright.

**Thoreau, Henry David** (1817–1862), individualistic American writer, philosopher, and naturalist.

**Tidwell, Mike,** acclaimed Washington, D.C., travel writer.

**Tito, Dennis,** 60-year-old California millionaire who became the first space tourist when he voyaged to the International Space Station on the Russian space shuttle Soyuz.

**Tolkien, J. R. R.** (1892–1973), South African–born British medieval scholar, philologist, and fantasy writer.

**Toole, John Kennedy** (1937–1969), posthumously published, brilliantly inventive novelist.

**Toth, Susan Allen,** American essayist and travel writer.

**Tournier, Paul,** French psychiatrist and writer.

**Turner, Charles,** writer of historical fiction.

**Twain, Mark** (1835–1910), pen name of Samuel Clemens, American humorist and world traveler.

**Tyler, Anne** (1941– ), American novelist best known for her depictions of middle-class family life.

**Verne, Jules** (1828–1905), French writer of fantastical adventure.

**Voltaire, François Marie Arouet de** (1694–1778), French *philosophe,* author, and scathing genius of literary and intellectual history.

**Walden, Dr. John,** American professor, medical doctor, writer, and jungle traveler.

**Walpole, Horace, 4th Earl of Orford** (1717–1797), English novelist and letter writer.

**Warburton, Eliot,** somewhat arch mid-19th-century Irish barrister and travel writer.

**Waugh, Evelyn Arthur St. John** (1903–66), English satirist.

**Watkins, Susan M.,** upstate New York writer of nonfiction.

**Welty, Eudora** (1909–2001), Southern short-story writer and novelist.

**Wheeler, Sara,** British travel writer, editor, and columnist.

**White, E. B.** (1899–1985), American writer of essays and children's literature.

**White, Edmund,** contemporary novelist and nonfiction writer.

**White, Randy Wayne,** multitalented columnist, travel writer, mystery writer, and former fly-fishing guide.

**Whitman, Walt** (1819–1892), unconventional New York poet.

**Williams, Hugo** (1942– ), British journalist, poet, and travel writer.

**Wodehouse, P. G.** (1881–1975), Anglo-American novelist and humorist best known for his satirical depiction of the English upper classes.

**Wolfe, Thomas** (1900–1938), richly descriptive Southern novelist.

**Wood, Michael,** British journalist, broadcaster, filmmaker, and traveler.

**Woodcock, George** (1912–1995) Canadian editor, poet, critic, travel writer, historian, philosopher, and essayist.

# Works Cited

Douglas Adams
  *Dirk Gently's Holistic Detective Agency* (1987)
  *The Hitchhiker's Guide to the Galaxy* (1979)
  *Mostly Harmless* (1992)

Philip Andrew Adams
  *Australian Age* 10 September 1983

Fred Allen
  Introduction to Art Buchwald's *Paris After Dark* (1954)

Martin Amis
  "Emergency Landing," *Soho Square II* (1989)

Jean Paul Aron
  *New York Times* 4 August 1986

*Aspinall's Pocket Guide to the West Indies* (1907)

Jane Austen
*Northanger Abbey* (1818)

Sir Francis Bacon
*Marguerite,* Sonnet No. 27
"On Travel" (1597)

Karl Baedecker
*The Eastern Alps: Handbook for Travellers* (1883)
*Egypt and the Sûdân: Handbook for Travellers* (1914)
*Palestine and Syria: Handbook for Travellers* (1906)
*Southern France: Handbook for Travellers* (1907)
*Switzerland: Handbook for Travellers* (1899)

Russell Baker
*New York Times* 5 November 1986

Sarah Ballard
*Sports Illustrated* 1 October 1984

Lord Baltimore
*A Tour to the East* (1767)

Bill Barich
*Traveling Light: A Year of Wandering from California to England and Tuscany and Back Again* (1984)

Dave Barry
*Dave Barry Does Japan* (1992)

Hilaire Belloc
*The Path to Rome* (1902)

Eleanor R. Belmont
*The Fabric of Memory* (1957)

Charles Berlitz
*Passport to the World: The 80 Key Words You Need to Communicate in 25 Languages* (1991)

The Bible, King James Version

Isabella Bird
*The Golden Chersonese and the Way Thither* (1883)
*Unbeaten Tracks in Japan* (1880)

Erma Bombeck
*When You Look Like Your Passport Photo, It's Time to Go Home* (1997)

Rupert Brooke
*Letter From America* (1916)

Bill Bryson

*I'm a Stranger Here Myself: Notes on Returning to America After 20 Years* (1999)

*In a Sunburned Country* (2000)

*A Walk in the Woods: Rediscovering America on the Appalachian Trail* (1998)

John Bunyan

*The Pilgrim's Progress* (1678)

Sir Richard Burton

*Personal Narrative of a Pilgrimage to Al-Madinah and Meccah* (1855–6)

Colonel Fred Burnby

*A Ride to Khiva* (1877)

Tim Cahill

*Road Fever; A High-Speed Travelogue* (1991)

James M. Cain

*Double Indemnity* (1936)

Philip Caputo

Introduction to *Greater Nowheres: A Journey Through the Australian Bush* by Dave Finkelstein and Jack London (1988)

Dave Carty
> *Born Again at the Laundromat: And Other Visions of the New West* (1992)

Bruce Chatwin
> *In Patagonia* (1977)
> *What Am I Doing Here* (1989)

Bruce Chatwin and Paul Theroux
> *Nowhere is a Place: Travels in Patagonia* (1985)

Geoffrey Chaucer
> The General Prologue, *The Canterbury Tales* (c. 1386)

John Cheever
> "The Bella Lingua" (1982)

Thurston Clarke
> *Equator: A Journey* (1988)

Tony Cohan
> *On Mexican Time: A New Life in San Miguel* (2000)

Louise Collis
> *Memoirs of a Medieval Woman: The Life and Times of Margery Kempe* (1964)

Joseph Conrad
*The Congo Diary* (1902)

James Fenimore Cooper
*The Last of the Mohicans* (1826)

Malcolm Cowle
*Exile's Return* (1934)

Mable Sharman Crawford (c. 1830–1860)
"Through Algeria," *Maiden Voyages: Writings of Women Travelers* (1993)

Michael Crichton
*Travels* (1988)

William Henry Crosse, M.D.
*Medical Hints* (1906)

Tom Cunliffe
*Good Vibrations: Coast to Coast on a Harley* (2001)

Alexandra David-Néel
*My Journey to Llasa* (1927)

Robyn Davidson
*Tracks* (1980)

Daniel Defoe
*Tour Thro' the Whole of Great Britain* (1724–26)

Charles de Gaulle
*Newsweek* 1 October 1962

Charles Dickens
*American Notes* (1842)
*Pictures From Italy* (1846)

Monica Dickens
"A Modern Dickens Writes about Returning to the Land of Her Great-Grandfather," *Christian Science Monitor* 13 March 1986

Fyodor Dostoevsky
"The Crocodile" (1865)
*The Gambler* (1867)
*The Idiot* (1868)

Charles Montagu Doughty
*Travels in Arabia Deserta* (1888)

Robin Douglas-Home
"Scotland: The Dour and the Beautiful," *Vogue* 15 Apr 1964

Sir Arthur Conan Doyle
*The Lost World* (1912)

Theodore Dreiser
*A Traveler at Forty* (1913)

Lawrence Durrell
*Bitter Lemons* (1957)

Amelia B. Edwards
*A Thousand Miles Up the Nile* (1877)

Ralph Waldo Emerson
*Journals* (1833)

Julian Evans
*Transit in Venus: Travels in the Pacific* (1992)

Temple Fielding
*Fielding's Guide to Europe* (1963)

Patrick Leigh Fermor
*A Time of Gifts* (1977)

Peter Fleming
*Brazilian Adventure* (1933)
*One's Company* (1934)

Benjamin Franklin
    *Poor Richard's Almanack* (1736)

Lucinda Franks
    "Thousands Ineptly Get Away from It All," *New York Times* 30
        August 1975

Michael Frayn
    "The Long Straight," *Great Railway Journeys of the World* (1981)

John Foster Fraser
    *Round the World on a Wheel* (1899)

Keath Fraser
    *Bad Trips* (1991)

Otto Friedrich
    *Time* 22 April 1985

Christopher Fry
    *The Lady's Not For Burning* (1948)

Thomas Fuller
    *Gnomologia* (1732)

Sir Francis Galton
    *The Art of Travel* (1867)

Martha Gellhorn
  *Travels with Myself and Another* (1978)

Georgie Ann Geyer
  *Waiting for Winter to End: An Extraordinary Journey Through Soviet Central Asia* (1994)

Johann Wolfgang von Goethe in 1786
  *Italian Journey* (1961)

William Golding
  *An Egyptian Journal* (1985)

Kenneth Grahame
  *The Wind in the Willows* (1908)

Graham Greene
  *Another Mexico* (1939)
  *The Stamboul Train* (1932)
  *Travels with My Aunt* (1969)
  *Ways of Escape* (1980)

John Groth
  *Studio Asia* (1952)

John Gunther
  *Inside Africa* (1953)

Richard Halliburton
  *The Glorious Adventure* (1927)

Gerald Hanley
  *The Journey Homeward* (1961)

Thomas Hardy
  *Far From the Madding Crowd* (1874)

Augustus J. C. Hare
  *North-Eastern France* (1890)

Eddy L. Harris
  *Mississippi Solo: A River Quest* (1988)

Tony Hawks
  *Round Ireland with a Fridge* (1998)

William Least Heat-Moon
  *Blue Highways: A Journey Into America* (1982)

Ernest Hemingway
  *A Moveable Feast* (1964)
  *The Sun Also Rises* (1926)

O. Henry
"Roads of Destiny" (1909)

Susana Herrera
*Mango Elephants in the Sun: How Life in an African Village Let Me Be in My Skin* (2000)

Jamake Highwater
*Journey to the Sky* (1978)

James Hilton
*Lost Horizon* (1933)

Edward Hoagland
*The Tugman's Passage* (1982)

Homer
*The Odyssey* (c. 700 B.C.)

Tony Horwitz
*One for the Road: An Outback Adventure* (1987)

Mrs. C. E. Humphries
*Manners for Women* (1897)

Lindsay Hunt
*Fodor's Exploring Ireland* (2001)

Aldous Huxley
    *Along the Road* (1925)

Elspeth Huxley
    *The Flame Trees of Thika* (1959)

Pico Iyer
    "First Person Middle East: The Worry Zone," *Conde Nast Traveler* May 2001
    *Global Soul: Jet Lag, Shopping Malls, and the Search for Home* (2000)

Henry James
    *The American* (1877)
    *English Hours* (1888)
    *A Little Town in France* (1884)

Peter Jenkins
    *Along the Edge of America* (1995)

Jerome K. Jerome
    *Three Men on a Bummel* (1900)

H. H. Johnston
    *Hints on Outfits* (1889)

Tristan Jones
*Encounters of a Wayward Sailor* (1991)

Elisha Kent Kane, M.D.
*Arctic Explorations* (1853)

Joe Kane
*Running the Amazon* (1989)

MacKinlay Kantor
*The Children Sing* (1973)

Robert D. Kaplan
*Balkan Ghosts: A Journey Through History* (1997)

Mary Karr
*Cherry* (2000)

Carolyn Keene
*The Secret of the Old Clock* (1930)

Jack Kerouac
*Big Sur* (1962)
"Big Trip to Europe," *Lonesome Traveler* (1960)
*The Dharma Bums* (1958)
*On the Road* (1959)
"The Vanishing Hobo," *Lonesome Traveler* (1960)

Ken Kesey, with Ken Babbs
*Last Go Round: A Dime Western* (1994)

A. W. Kinglake
*Eothen* (1844)

Mary Kingsley
*Travels in West Africa* (1897)

Rudyard Kipling
*Just-So Stories* (1902)

Frances G. Knight
*New York Herald Tribune* 21 February 1957

Hans Koning
*International Herald Tribune* 15 November 1985

Milan Kundera
*Life Is Elsewhere* (1973)

Charles Kuralt
*A Life on the Road* (1990)

Osbert Lancaster
*Classical Landscape with Figures* (1947)

Doug Lansky
*Up the Amazon Without a Paddle* (1999)

Philip Larkin
*New York Times* 3 December 1985

Laurie Lee
*As I Walked Out One Midsummer Morning* (1969)

Ian Littlewood
*Sultry Climates: Travel and Sex Since the Grand Tour* (2001)

Andy Logan
*The New Yorker* 9 April 1984

Susan Herrmann Loomis
*On the Rue Tatin: Living and Cooking in a French Town* (2001)

Anita Loos
*The New York Times* 26 April 1973

Hector MacQuarrie
*Tahiti Days* (1920)

Thomas Mallon
*New York Times* 21 June 1985

David Mamet
"A Family Vacation," *Writing in Restaurants* (1986)

Captain R. B. Marcy
*The Prairie and Overland Traveler* (1860)

Peter Matthiessen
*African Silences* (1991)

W. Somerset Maugham
"Honolulu," *The Trembling of a Leaf* (1921)

Gavin Maxwell
*A Reed Shaken by the Wind* (1957)

Frances Mayes
*Under the Tuscan Sun: At Home in Italy* (1997)

Peter Mayle
*Encore Provence: New Adventures in the South of France* (1999)

Simon Mayle
*The Burial Brothers: From New York to Rio in a '73 Cadillac Hearse* (1996)

Ruth McKenney
*Far, Far From Home* (1952)

Larry McMurtry
*The Desert Rose* (1983)
*Roads: Driving America's Great Highways* (2000)

Margaret Mead
*Coming of Age in Samoa* (1928)

Herman Melville
*Typee: A Romance of the South Seas* (1846)

James A. Michener
*The Drifters* (1971)

Miles Morland
*A Walk Across France* (1992)

Jan Morris (James Morris)
"It's OK to Stay at Home," *New York Times* 30 August 1985

Mary Morris
*Maiden Voyages: Writings of Women Travelers* (1993)

Thomas More
"Of the Travelling of the Utopians," *Utopia* (1516)

Fynes Moryson
*An Itinerary Written by Fynes Moryson, Gent.* (1617)

*Murray's Handbook for Travellers in the Ionian Islands, Greece, Turkey, Asia Minor and Constantinople* (1840)

Jan Myrdal
*The Silk Road* (1980)

Sandra L. Myres
*Westering Women and the Frontier Experience, 1800–1815* (1982)

V. S. Naipaul
*An Area of Darkness* (1964)

Craig Nelson
*Let's Get Lost: Adventures in the Great Wide Open* (1999)

Sylvaine Rouy Neves
*New York Times* 30 September 1984

Eric Newby
*Departures and Arrivals* (1999)
*Slowly Down the Ganges* (1966)

John Julius Norwich
*A Taste for Travel* (1985)

Thomas Nugent
*The Grand Tour* (1749)

P. J. O'Roarke
*Holidays in Hell* (1988)

Cynthia Ozick
"Enchanters at First Encounter," *New York Times* 17 March 1985

Michael Palin
*Around the World in Eighty Days* (1989)
"Confessions of a Train Spotter," *Great Railway Journeys of the World* (1981)
*Pole to Pole: North to South by Camel, River Raft, and Balloon* (1992)

Michael Paterniti
  *Driving Mr. Albert: A Trip Across America with Einstein's Brain* (2000)

David Pauly
  "Airport '84: Stalled Out," *Newsweek* 30 July 1984

Robert Young Pelton
  *The World's Most Dangerous Places* (1997)

S. J. Perelman
  *The Swiss Family Perelman* (1950)

Marco Polo
  *The Travels of Marco Polo* (c. 1298)

Ann E. Porter
  "The Banishment of Peddlers," *Godey's* 37, October 1848

V. S. Pritchett
  *At Home and Abroad* (1989)
  *London Perceived* (1962)

Jonathan Raban
  *Old Glory: An American* (1981)
  *Passage to Juneau: A Sea and Its Mirages* (1999)

Rudolf Erich Raspe
*Travels of Baron Münchausen* (1786)

Tom Robbins
*Another Roadside Attraction* (1972)
*Even Cowgirls Get the Blues* (1976)
*Half Asleep in Frog Pajamas* (1994)
*Still Life with Woodpecker* (1980)

Eric Robson
"Changing Trains," *Great Railway Journeys of the World* (1981)

Robert Alden Rubin
*On the Beaten Track: An Appalachian Pilgrimage* (2000)

John Russell
*New York Times* 4 August 1977

Vita Sackville-West
*Passenger to Teheran* (1926)
*Twelve Days* (1928)

Dorothy L. Sayers
*Busman's Honeymoon* (1937)

Rob Schultheis
> *Fool's Gold: Lives, Loves, and Misadventures in the Four Corners Country* (2000)

"The Seven Voyages of Sinbad the Sailor"
> *The Arabian Nights* (c. 1000)

William Shakespeare
> *As You Like It* (c. 1599)

Igor Sikorsky
> *New York Times* 13 September 1959

Georges Simenon
> *The White Horse Inn* (1938)

Ted Simon
> *The Gypsy in Me: From Germany to Romania in Search of Youth, Truth, and Dad* (1997)
> *Jupiter's Travels: Four Years Around the World on a Triumph* (1979)
> *Riding High* (1984)

Captain Joshua Slocum
> *Sailing Alone Around the World* (1900)

Freya Stark
> *Alexander's Path* (1958)
> *Baghdad Sketches* (1932)
> *The Coast of Incense* (1953)

Ronald Steel
> "Life in the Last 50 Years," *Esquire* June 1983

John Steinbeck
> *Travels with Charley* (1962)

Laurence Sterne
> *A Sentimental Journey Through France and Italy* (1768)

Stuart Stevens
> *Malaria Dreams: An African Adventure* (1989)
> *Night Train to Turkestan: Modern Adventures Along China's Ancient Silk Road* (1988)

Robert Louis Stevenson
> *Travels with a Donkey in the Cévennes* (1879)

Rick Steves
> *Europe Through the Back Door* (1998)

Chris Stewart
*Driving Over Lemons: An Optimist in Andalucía* (1999)

Jonathan Swift
*Gulliver's Travels* (1726)
*My Lady's Lamentation* (1728)

Alfred, Lord Tennyson
"Ulysses" (1842)

Tiziano Tenzani
*A Fortune Teller Told Me: Earthbound Adventures in the Far East* (1997)

Captain Philip Thicknesse
*A Year's Journey Through France and Part of Spain* (1777)

Paul Theroux
*Fresh Air Fiend: Travel Writings, 1985–2000* (2000)

Walter Thesinger
*Arabian Sands* (1959)
*The Marsh Arabs* (1964)

Brian Thompson
"Deccan," *Great Railway Journeys of the World* (1981)

Mike Tidwell
> *Amazon Stranger: A Rainforest Chief Battles Big Oil* (1996)
> *In the Mountains of Heaven: Tales of Adventure on Six Continents* (2000)

John Kennedy Toole
> *A Confederacy of Dunces* (1980)

Susan Allen Toth
> *England for All Seasons* (1997)
> *My Love Affair with England: A Traveler's Memoirs* (1992)

Paul Tournier
> *The Meaning of Persons* (1957)

Charles Turner
> *The Celebrant* (1982)

Mark Twain
> *Following the Equator: A Journey Around the World* (1897)
> *Innocents Abroad* (1869)
> "Letters to Satan" (1923)
> *A Tramp Abroad* (1880)

Anne Tyler
> *The Accidental Tourist* (1985)

Jules Verne
>*Around the World in Eighty Days* (1873)
>*From the Earth to the Moon* (1865)

Voltaire
>*Candide* (1759)

John Walden
>*Jungle Travel and Survival* (2001)

Horace Walpole
>*The Letters of Horace Walpole* (1891)

Eliot Warburton
>*The Crescent and the Cross* (1845)

Evelyn Waugh
>"Scott-King's Modern Europe" (1947)
>*Waugh in Abyssinia* (1935)
>*When the Going Was Good* (1934)

Eudora Welty
>*One Writer's Beginnings* (1984)

Sara Wheeler
>*Terra Incognita: Travels to the Antarctic* (1996)
>*Travels In A Thin Country: A Journey Through Chile* (1999)

E. B. White
*One Man's Meat* (1943)

Edmund White
*The Flâneur: A Stroll through the Paradoxes of Paris* (2001)

Randy Wayne White
*The Sharks of Lake Nicaragua: True Tales of Adventure, Travel, and Fishing* (1999)

Hugo Williams
"La Folie Anglaise," *All the Time in the World* (1966)

P. G. Wodehouse
*The Luck of the Bodkins* (1935)

Thomas Wolfe
*Look Homeward Angel* (1929)

Michael Wood
"Zambezi Express," *Great Railway Journeys of the World* (1981)

George Woodcock
"My Worst Journey," *Bad Trips* (1991)

# Index